Wandering Ecologies

A Plantsman's Journey

The Landscape Architecture of Charles Anderson

Edited by Julie Decker

This edition published in September 2011

Design Media Publishing Limited
20/F Manulife Tower
169 Electric Rd, North Point
Hong Kong
Tel: 00852-28672587
Fax: 00852-25050411
E-mail: Kevinchoy@designmediahk.com
www.designmediahk.com

Editing: Julie Decker
Proofreading: Maggie Wang
Design/Layout: Chunling Yang

ISBN 978-988-19739-6-2

Printed in China

Wandering Ecologies

A Plantsman's Journey

The Landscape Architecture of Charles Anderson

Edited by Julie Decker

DESIGN MEDIA PUBLISHING LIMITED

CHARLES ANDERSON | ATELIER PS

Landscape Architecture Urbanism
www.charlesanderson-atelierps.com

EDITOR | Julie Decker, Ph.D., is a project manager for Trailer Art Center, Director of the International Gallery of Contemporary Art, and a frequent guest art curator at the Anchorage Museum. She is also an instructor of art history for the University of Alaska. She holds a doctorate in contemporary art history, a master's degree in arts administration, and bachelor degrees in fine art and journalism. Decker has authored numerous articles and publications on the art and architecture of Alaska, including John Hoover: Art & Life, Icebreakers: Alaska's Most Innovative Artists, Found & Assembled in Alaska, Quonset: Metal Living for a Modern Age, Modern North: Architecture on the Frozen Edge and True North: Contemporary Architecture of Alaska. As an artist, she has participated in numerous solo and group exhibitions, working in painting, sculpture and photography.

ACKNOWLEDGMENTS

To my Family: my wife of 22 years and three children who put up with the chaotic but poetic approach to life and work. Especially all the love, joy and laughter they always bring to each and every day. To my Mother and Father for giving me a shot at life and always being there to listen and encourage me even in my moving far away to Cambridge to attend graduate school. To my sisters who are an unending source of adventure while still living in my home state of North Dakota. To my big brother who never thought that the best was really good enough until his much too early death in the spring of 2008.

To the endless number of studio mates and colleagues over the years who have collaborated on amazing projects in challenging times. Especially Sheri Olson, FAIA, for her guidance in "the story", and to Julie Decker, PH.D., for taking on the role of editing and distilling this story into a cohesive journey. Julie's artistic nature imbibes all that she chooses to do with an elegance and simplicity that is evident here.

Finally to the Great Spirit, who gave me the eyes of an Eagle, the strength of a Bear, the stamina of a Buffalo, and the the yearning of Vincent van Gogh.

CHARLES ANDERSON

CONTENTS

INTRODUCTION

Water feature at University of Oregon, John E. Jaqua Academic Center for Student Athletes

It's hard to explain why, but I always look forward to working with Charles...I know he's talented and his landscapes provide beautiful settings for our structures... but it's more than that. It's his personality, his curiosity, his enjoyment of life. Working as a designer is like living your whole life exploring a treasured hobby. It's a serious life commitment, yet we often mix friendship and fun into our work process.

Like Charles, I believe in collaboration and I see our disciplines, architecture and landscape architecture, as two parts of a harmonious whole – the environments we create. In my architecture, the indoor/outdoor visual flow is often a theme, making the landscape an extension of the architectural space. Charles appreciates that and looks at his landscapes as part of the indoor, as well as outdoor, experience.

Collaborations work best when goals are in sync and when there's a lot of mutual respect. That explains why Charles and I find our collaborations to be so rewarding.

In our collaborations Charles always takes us beyond the project in two important directions. First, he makes us smile, whether it's his buffalo shirt or some amazing story. Second, he takes us on an exploration, often through those stories. Meanings go beyond the task at hand and take our efforts to another level. At the Whatcom Museum in Bellingham, Charles envisioned a "Garden of the Ancients" where an old Ginkgo tree would befriend an existing Sequoia tree – both were around when the dinosaurs roamed the earth. In a project in Denver, Charles created a home for the neighborhood fox, complete with nearby bunny sculptures to keep him entertained.

Charles is fun. Charles is committed. Charles is tenacious. He stands up for what he thinks is right. Charles brings his curiosity and love of life to everything he does. The work he creates is far richer for it. His beautiful landscapes will give back that richness for generations to come.

—Jim Olson, FAIA
Olson Kundig Architects

Wake 2004, Richard Serra at The Gardens of the Olympic Sculpture Park

INTRODUCTION

Chuck Anderson came to work with me in the last of the 1980's, after his persistent professional pursuit. After a month or so, the name Chuck was increasingly inappropriate and I proposed that he become Charles. That stuck and that's who he's been ever since. In the office he wasn't afraid to pester me, in fact I once told him he was like a mosquito; he's on one side, you swat at him and he just moves to the other side. A tenacious fellow indeed, with quixotic praise, he is one maven maverick!

For months Charles bugged me to get him a computer - for some reason he was drawn to that technology. After Charles left to open his own office, we lost touch for nearly a decade. Charles had established his reputation when I invited him (and his laptop) to collaborate on the 2008 Beijing Olympics competition. We were teamed with XWHO, a Chinese design company. In Beijing, Charles and I were a little factory of drawings and ideas that made our hosts laugh often. We placed second, but opened up a trialogue that is even more rewarding.

His work is a lot about plants and sculpting the earth. He is a champion for the profession of landscape architecture and shares my view of its importance. In a time where landscape architects are joining other design offices, usually architects or engineers, I cannot foresee a time when Charles will let go of the challis of our profession's individuality - I cannot see him give up on mother earth as the center of his perceived universe.

The reader should note that Charles Anderson's insectivorciferous powers are unabated. He solicited a few words on "approach to design" or a "world view of landscape architecture". So here is a credo written when Charles worked with me:

The Cosmos is an experiment
The Universe is a park
The Earth is a pleasure ground
Nature is the theater
The Landscape is our stage
Let us write the script
Direct the play
and embrace the audience
with compassion and joy
for LIFE

—Rich Haag, FASLA
Richard Haag Associates

A Plantsman's Journey

By Charles Anderson, FASLA

"We take a handful of sand from the endless landscape of awareness around us and call that handful of sand the world."
—*Zen and the Art of Motorcycle Maintenance by Alan Pirsig*

A few days before Christmas 2007, I found myself 35,000 feet in the air, en route to North Dakota, my birthplace; not for the holidays, but for a new project at the International Peace Garden. After several decades of work around the world, my fiftieth year brought me full circle. The project is ironic; much of my career has been anything but peaceful.

The first 20 years of this plantsman's journey centered in Jamestown, North Dakota, in a valley surrounded by prairie and farmlands. As a teenager I earned money by working the landscape; sometimes as a farm hand, but mostly mowing grass, laying prairie sod and doing earthwork. In 1978, at the age of 21, I completed my first public landscape design for the Jamestown Holiday Inn, part of a government initiative for urban renewal.

I had been trained at the North Dakota State School of Forestry in Bottineau, where I learned to corral my restless energy, hone my graphic talent and develop a penchant for shaping the landscape. I had other priorities, too - my motorcycle and car were two of them. While I didn't see words like others do because of dyslexia, I did have an uncanny ability to remember the Latin names of plants.

Later, at North Dakota State University in Fargo, I met my first landscape architect, Professor Ron Zuber, who became the most important person in my developing career. Without his influence, I'm sure I would have stayed with horticulture rather than being drawn into the metaphysics of design. Zuber also prodded me to read Pirsig's Zen and the Art of Motorcycle Maintenance. I learned about "quality" and began my endless pursuit of my personal version of Pirsig's Phaedrus. Unlike Pirsig's, a ghost of his former life, Phaedra is an energy that leads me through my career, beckoning me to follow and pass through each threshold to a new and untested place. Similarly, Zuber suggested that as you move from place to place, you must recognize that in each new place you will see what you want to see. "Keep going my friend, keep going," he said.

I kept going, arriving in Pullman, Washington to further my studies in late spring 1978. Pullman was a city of high-rise dormitory buildings set in wheat fields and surrounded by mountains. To me, the Palouse region of Washington resembled a North Dakota farm and prairie landscape on steroids. Architecture became a focus for my studies at Washington State University. I met other sage professors there;

Professor Richard Rosine was one, although he didn't take me under his wing. Instead, he watched and said a fewprecious things at critical times.

My first year was nearly cut short by the eruption of Mount St. Helens on May 18, 1980. Walking through the inch of ash that settled within a several hundred-mile radius of the volcano, I could not have dreamed that I would someday be the lead design for the newly-formed Mount St. Helens National Volcanic Monument, or that it would earn me my second national design award.

My second year in Pullman introduced me to Fritz Steiner, who mandated a respect for nature and a collaborative design process that included the sciences. Professor Ken Brooks pushed me in the area of planting design and taught me the importance of good landscape structure. I developed my own styles of rendering from his classes; using magic markers that made the flat paper three-dimensional. I learned about LeCorbusier and became fascinated with the simplicity, boldness, and mystic proportions of his work, and his ability to link art, architecture and landscape.

In 1981 the country was in the grip of a recession, but I was able to get a job offer from Moriece & Gary Landscape Architects in Cambridge. I immersed myself in the cultural richness of New England and took advantage of art museums, concerts and lectures. I also bounced around, working for several landscape architecture firms like a mercenary, including the offices of Bill Pressley and Pat Loheed. I moved east to attend graduate school and decided this was the time to apply. Harvard waitlisted me for the landscape architecture program, but Penn offered me a chance to study under Ian McHarg and learn directly from him about designing with nature. I caught a glimpse of Phaedra's ankle, this time a portal opened to Philadelphia. I left Boston looking over my shoulder, sensing there was unfinished business and suspecting I would return.

My semester at Penn was spectacular because of the classes that I took in architecture and Mcharg's studio. In one seminar I heard Buckminster Fuller, Edmund Bacon, McHarg and numerous other philosophers, writers and poets. One class introduced me to the idea of using native plants and, in hindsight; it was this course that played the largest role in determining a very central focus of my career. Professors from Andropogon Associates, a Philadelphia landscape architecture firm, helped me understand that planting design that is in tune with natural systems is pivotal to all meaningful and contextual landscapes.

At mid-semester I found out that Harvard accepted me into their program for the following fall and I decided to go. When I informed McHarg, he told me I would regret going to Harvard despite it being his alma mater. I didn't know it then, but his words were prophetic, to be realized twenty years later.

I spent the summer before starting Harvard at home in North Dakota, working with my father and for Galpin Associates, a small landscape architecture office in Bismarck. In my conversations with my father we discussed the merits and cost of graduate school versus getting to work. It made sense to settle down, but there again was the ankle of Phaedra, this time a more familiar portal back to Boston and a new set of challenges. The decision was complicated when my father suffered a heart attack that summer. But I had to go on with this journey.

My time at Harvard was remarkable. I immersed myself in design, taking classes in stage sets, art and architecture. I learned from Jerzy Soltan, an architect who worked closely with LeCorbusier, and Peter Walker, who taught me to design from a strong position and to defend it with clarity and purpose. From him I also learned the value of the parti and the importance of the pursuit the "one liner", although there could be any number of them in a design. His design approach to studio was from the view of a modernist, a minimalist, and an artist. I took a very memorable joint studio with Frank Gehry, Claes Oldenburg, and Martha Schwartz. But the professor that influenced me the most was Cherie Kluesing, who brought artists and landscape architects together in small gatherings for presentations and discussions. Through her I met Richard Haag, who spoke about mother earth with a passion that I had heard from no one else. I also met James Turrell and went to work for him on a light and dance installation called "Severe Clear", in a landmark athletic building at Radcliff. By inviting so many artists to share perspectives, Kluesing demystified the artists and made them approachable. It was liberating to learn that they, too, were driven by their own pursuits of Phaedra.

Graduation day came. I longed for the west, for a place free from so many rules, from so much tradition. I caught sight of Phaedra again, this time her ankle just passing through a portal to work with James Turrell on his Roden Crater project in Arizona, where I arrived in the summer of 1985. I reported to work at Turrell's studio in Flagstaff and early the next day we headed out in four-wheel-drives and trucks on a fifteen-mile journey to the crater where Turrell was developing Skystones, the reshaping of an extinct volcanic cinder cone into an astronomical observatory. I didn't realize until after I arrived that I would not be paid for my labor so after one glorious night at the crater I left to find a paying job. I spent the next two years in Tucson, purging east coast pretensions from my veins. I soon saw limitations for designers in this conservative community but it was there I met my soul mate and wife, Nancy. Together we traveled to Boston where I returned to Moriece & Gary's office. After only two months, I realized I couldn't conform to life back East. On a sun-starved February day in 1987, Nancy and I arrived in Seattle to see if the Northwest would be a match.

After the scorching sun and colors of the desert, Seattle's cold moisture soaked deep into our bones and our psyche. How could there be so much green and so little light? I began work in a small landscape architecture office for Tom Rengstorf. We worked on multifamily residential communities, with landscapes that often had themes, in places designed to offer a lifestyle with resort-like amenities, often in environmentally sensitive sites. Nancy accepted a position with an airline and for ten years we took every opportunity we could afford to travel abroad, seeing new places, looking for new ways to solve traditional landscape issues and confirming the existence of universal design truths. I learned one thing, although slowly: I didn't have to cross the country to pursue variety. From its position on the Pacific Rim, Seattle provided opportunities to work in faraway places with exotic challenges. This time Phaedra morphed into multiple portals to places throughout the U.S. and Asia.

With a new position at EDAW, Inc, I entered the design challenge for the national volcanic monument at Mount St. Helens, one of the first high-profile design opportunities I had an opportunity to lead. Mt. St. Helens is one of the most sinister and yet beautiful places on the planet. In spite of the great work at EDAW, I decided to join Rich Haag, to learn from a master plantsman. I was a confident designer but I still saw plants as embellishment of architecture. Working with Rich,

I began to look closely at the character of each plant and saw the way a collection of a single species influences the characteristics and behaviors of a single plant. He grew his favorite trees in his own nursery and his trees have a unique character, as do his designs. Haag advocates "non-striving", letting the spirit of design take you where it must, to allow the essence of an idea to emerge. I left his office much earlier than I should have, mainly because he refused to get me a computer; he wanted me to draw. We parted ways on difficult terms but our paths would cross again.

I briefly returned to Arizona to work with Gage Davis, an architect with legendary site sensibilities. The projects were primarily theme-based resort design, but he left me with an idea that became a foundation for my future work as a plantsman. It came out of the time Gage and I would sit together on Saturday mornings and I would draw while he would comment on my work, sometimes pointing out a fatal flaw in the design. Once, he said I needed a tree - not just any tree but the tree. "One like the great olive trees in Italy," he'd say. "One that would completely dominate its place and bring order to the design." Every person needs a mentor and every garden needs the tree.

Phaedra soon teased me back to the Northwest, this time to start my own office. Anderson Ray Brown opened for business in August of 1994. Stephen Ray, a master detailer and construction documents person, and Walt Brown, a computer wizard, joined me for this enterprise. Some of our first projects were ones that followed me from Gage Davis's office, but we also had one of Seattle's philanthropists, Anne Lennartz, as a client. Fascinated by industrial landscapes, I learned about plans to demolish the defunct Satsop Nuclear Power Plant in Western Washington and return the land to forests. I arranged a visit to the power plant and drew up plans to keep the cooling towers and create a larger version of Seattle's Gasworks Park. We became part of the design team charged with the creation of a Satsop Development Park. The sublime beauty of the enormous towers juxtaposed against the adjacent forest and sky is unforgettable.

Anderson & Ray (Walt Brown left in 1995) grew to a staff of seven and we were quickly establishing ourselves with native plants projects. At the time we called this genre of work urban ecology, but today it may be more like landscape urbanism. The foundation for this began with my experience in Arizona, where the use of native plants was mandated and becoming mainstream. There, the rigors of an arid landscape led to a systems approach to design often headed by civil engineers. It was reinforced at EDAW on the Mount St. Helens project where indigenous - but not always native - plants for restoration had to come from within the monument boundaries.

All of this gelled on the day that I met Anne Lennartz. She announced that she wanted to work with someone who understood the importance of using native plants in the city and who could create drainage systems and landforms that could support a diverse plant, wildlife and human habitat. Anne was from Iowa, but she reminded me of someone from New England. She was often seen with books in her arms and peered out over her reading glasses with a stare that made you feel like an explanation was in order. I became her designer of choice for several significant parks and "leftover" urban open spaces within Seattle, which would eventually be the first urban ecological restoration projects to win an American Society of Landscape Architects (ASLA) National Design Award in 2004. Anne was a loyal client and a dear friend who had an enormous impact on the direction and emphasis of my career.

In 1997, Stephen Ray and I began talking to landscape artist Kathryn Gustafson about joining us. Kathryn had recently returned to the Northwest after twenty years of working in Europe, most of those years spent in France. She had no U.S. office and we began to work together on projects. One day she told us that she had been asked to participate in a paid competition for the one-acre roof garden called The Arthur Ross Terrace, on top of a new parking garage at the American Museum of Natural History in New York. We won with a design based on the constellations. Simultaneously, we began work on the South Coast Plaza in Costa Mesa, California. Kathryn was hired as lead designer and Anderson & Ray as landscape architect of record, providing complete services through construction administration. I monitored the work as it progressed, mainly looking for health, safety and welfare issues and constructability. This was much less of a design collaboration than the other projects and plans to form a joined studio fell away. I was resistant to losing my identity to Kathryn; the difficult but exciting plaza project was the last we would do together. But life was coming together in other ways. Nancy and I were joined by Luna, a Labrador Retriever, and three daughters, first-born Natalie and twins Isabel and Kira. The role of designer took on a new dimension with a family. I reconnected with the child in me through them.

On a gray day in the early winter of 2000, the principals at EDAW asked Anderson & Ray to merge with their company. I began a new position with an old partner. Work was exciting, with a design phase for the new Stapleton Central Park Project in Denver and numerous projects in Northern California. The association lasted eight months, but soon I saw Phaedra and left to form my own new design studio. This time it would be Charles Anderson Landscape Architecture (CALA); no partners, no co-conspirators and no confusion. The studio officially began on the day before the falling of the World Trade Center Towers, an ominous beginning.

The studio would forge a balance between ecology and "big idea" design. We merged disciplined minimalist design principles with the poetry and complexity of life in all its forms. Landscape urbanism was evolving, too, but it seemed little more than a rebirth of post-modernism packaged in beautiful impressionistic graphics and too many new words. I preferred the term "urban ecology", an all-inclusive term for systems that includes every aspect of urban living.

In the fall of 2001 we joined the design team for the Seattle Art Museum's (SAM) new Olympic Sculpture Park. A few years earlier, I prepared plans for an interim landscape for the museum's recently purchased waterfront site. Weiss/Manfredi Architects, a New York-based firm, won the international competition to design the park. They proposed a reverse Z-shaped path to link the pieces of the site bisected by a road and railroad tracks. It was a great concept, but I saw the potential to add layers and depth. As landscape architect on the project, CALA graded the different precincts of the park, proposed an amphitheatre and a protective cove, provided the archetypal "mountain to sound" landscape metaphor, and selected the plants.

After design development and presentations were completed, a contract clause gave Weiss/Manfredi sole design credit for the project. CALA won a design award for the Park but Weiss/Manfredi did, too - an award from Harvard that did not identify the project design as collaborative. Frustrated with the lack of proper credit, I considered leaving Seattle and moving to my satellite Napa office. I didn't see Phaedra anywhere. There were financial struggles in the office, in part prompted by my stubbornness in the fight for public credit for our role on the Park. I just couldn't accept a lesser role. In my mind, I was thinking that I was defending the importance of landscape architecture in visual terms, as an art form, to the public and future clients.

In 2002, Richard Haag asked me to join him Xia of XWHO Design in the 2008 Olympics Design Competition in Beijing. This was an important development in my career; I was thrilled by an opportunity to work with Richard again and to visit China. I again looked to my mentor for guidance. Haag led by example and with not too much advice. We ate great food and worked feverishly on our competition entry. We did not win, but I found myself in the good graces of a maverick.

With a few public and painful exceptions, the vast majority of projects in the CALA office were successful collaborations with well-known architects. Jim Olson (of Olson Kundig Architects) collaborated with us on over a dozen projects over eight years. He sees the landscape the way I see architecture: as inseparable from the other. On our Tables of Water project, a prominent residence, I learned from Olson how the exterior of the building should grow into the house and the reverse; not just borrowed scenery but integrated elements. He had a mild but disciplined approach that any good Scandinavian could understand, with an eye to art and a love of the landscape.

Often the collaborations are intuitive, as it was in 2003 when I worked with British architect David Chipperfield on the expansion of the Anchorage Museum in Alaska. Before the design process had begun I was asked what I would do with the two-acre open space in front of the new museum. Thinking of the forest surrounding Anchorage, I told Chipperfield I would grab a bunch of trees and fling them in front of his building. He immediately loved the idea, glad that I was not proposing another element-filled American-style park. Instead, birch trees became architecture for defining "rooms", just like the new fritted silver-white glass of the Chipperfield's facade framed the building. His pragmatism met mine.

Carlos Zapata makes sculpture with his buildings. He approaches design with great bravado and appreciates the power of landscape as an integral part of architecture. In Hanoi, he proposed a glass building on a lake, conceived as an ascending dragon-a faceted glass building where our landscape metaphor completed the story. Here, our landscape becomes the progeny of the dragon, versed in a creation myth of the Vietnamese people. CALA also collaborated with Zapata on a waterfront project in Reno, Nevada, where he was proposing an elegant high-rise condominium development. Unfortunately, the development was adjacent to an unattractive parking garage. Zapata proposed to cover the 200-foot-high blight with landscape. The solution wars an eighteen-story tree wall, made up of a series of trays and native trees, a beautiful pairing of architecture and landscape.

The collaboration with Tadao Ando was unusual. We still have never met. He proposed an idea in email and I responded. He reacted to my thoughts, and then we agreed. It was unorthodox, but it worked. Maybe it is our shared love of LeCorbusier that allowed me to understand where he was going with his design for a small memorial chapel in Seattle.

When in 2007 Phaedra beckoned me to the International Peace Garden, I was reminded of my first visit to the site when I was eight years old. The Garden is centered on the 49th parallel on the border between Canada and the US. It is in the Turtle Mountains, an anomaly on North Dakota's otherwise vast prairie, and is matched in size only by Washington DC's mall and the great gardens of Versailles. The first major renovation since it was built in 1932 included the reconstruction of the sunken garden, a new interpretive center, a lodge and an international center for peace. This journey returned me to my homeland, to a place where my career began, as a designer of landscapes and a budding plantsman. My work is based on the ecological principles that belie the profession of landscape architecture, both the visceral and the actual. Richard Haag will be 86 years old soon. Maybe I will have three or four more decades to hone my craft as well. Maybe Phaedra will always lead me somewhere; I cannot say.

The phone did ring again recently with a new opportunity, this time towards Portland. Nike has an unbelievable project, which became a glass box in a glass box set on a plinth of black water, adjacent to a wedge of pure white birches. Here it just makes sense to pattern the living parts of landscape like nature… fragile, flexible, inspirational, and essential. There are always new projects that find their way into the studio. They come because of our commitment to a rich and living landscape, one positioned between the soil that nourishes and the fertility of our imaginations. My travels to Asia have opened my eyes to balance, not just in composition. The yin-yang I seek is one of contrasting elements or of complementary energy. Great art or architecture will not be great without an equally great setting; the reverse is not always true. This makes landscape the most important element of urban design.

This century will see a paradigm shift in the way in which landscape is viewed, much like one that the Hopi referred to as Kuwanlelenta-to make beautiful surroundings. Kuwanlelenta does not subscribe to the "en vogue" aspect of design, but, instead, acceptance of natural systems. Balance comes to an urban landscape when intensive high resource elements have a counterpoint as a filter for pollutants or storing carbon. A lawn area will be restricted to places that need turf and the other elements of the landscape mitigate those impacts, as meadows or planted places. Artistic expression always has a place in this landscape idiom. The most beautiful landscapes are those that espouse all forms of life from the birds, bugs, bunnies and surprises that reaffirm our connection to our simple yet complex biosphere. Robert Smithson created in Spiral Jetty a masterpiece of art and nature. Rooted as a conceptual design that is turned loose to the processes of nature, it has parallels to how the 21st-century landscape must be: a strong and beautiful composition that is allowed to evolve with the least effort and cost to our planet's nonrenewable resources, adding to a positive regeneration.

Maybe the Olympic Sculpture Park is a first timid step in this direction. The salvaging of old growth topsoil and use of native plants are steps in the right direction. Perhaps the stakeholders will see dying plants as a threat, a hazard and failure rather than as an opportunity provided by the beauty of the cycles of a dynamic living and dying landscape. I am drawn to the balance of these meadows, to the adjacent turf, to the wildlife that resides in urban habitat. Balance is achieved through education that allows for an ideal that is not idealized but is ideal for a sustainable existence.

This is a plantsman's journey toward acceptance of a living landscape, toward seizing the opportunity for balance. I imagine that one day our cities will again be graced with the native wildlife rather than the pigeons, rats and feral pets we accept as urban wildlife today.

Maybe looking back to humankind's earliest days are foolhardy. Maybe humankind's evolution is an unstoppable move away from a shared planet. Recently I looked through my living room window into my backyard with one of my daughters. We watched mesmerized as several different species of birds performed an opera. The birds were there because they knew the plants that we put there; they would come and know what to expect. They appreciate the habitat and we appreciate their visits. The 1980 eruption of Mount St. Helens eradicated a pristine mountain landscape in minutes, yet instantly life began the ecological process anew. The same can happen in our cities, but only with our help, with a renewed appreciation of the creatures with which we have evolved and with a determination to convert every rooftop, yard and piece of ground to shared habitat.

One wet spring morning, the broken-hearted voice of my mother awoke me. I was sure it was my father who had died. It wasn't; it was my older brother Doug, who pushed me the hardest of anyone in my childhood to achieve. He called me "Professor" and "Motor Mouth" because of my need to explain with zeal everything I learned. His passing leaves business between us unfinished, especially as we had become amused by our differences. I spoke at his wake and wore his Rush Limbaugh tie, like garlic to a vampire, but to me a symbol that even those with opposite views can find common ground in life and in death.

The economy of the world has taken a severe turn for the worse; in fact there is a true lack of confidence that we will get back to the bull excesses of the financial markets anytime soon. It is a good time to reconsider our direction as a nation and individuals who make up one world. Phaedra lead me to Phoenix, to the Sonoran Desert, to follow something intangible… a feeling that I was ready to try something in a new but familiar place. The valley of the sun has an unexplainable draw, one that has drawn independent-minded designers like Frank Lloyd Wright and Paolo Soleri. Arizona State University in Tempe is the creative heart of this vast urban landscape. The opportunity to teach at the school surfaced thanks to Kenneth Brooks, my professor from over twenty years ago.

My grandfather's name was Charles, too, I remember him for homesteading Indian land in South Dakota, for having seen the last remnant of wild buffalo herds, for being a pioneer like the Norseman of his ancestry. This familiar landscape will become what my Scandinavian ancestors called "new found land" because I see it again from the perspective of a middle-aged person's life experience. I wish my brother could have lived to hear my students call me "Professor".

Teaching in a university was a rewarding experience. The students seem thirsty for not just process but intent and philosophy. My second studio at Arizona State University included ten architects and five landscape architects. We tackled one of the most recognizable parts of the Valley of the Sun - Old Town Scottsdale. The students were assigned to read Zen and the Art of Motorcycle Maintenance. They eagerly plunged into preparation for a final presentation to a truly all-star cast that included Gage Davis, Will Bruder, Eric Mott, Kim Steel, and the local developer Fred Unger.

I have been quite vocal of my disapproval of the term landscape urbanism. Thinking that the idea of landscape as catalyst infrastructure was not a new idea or that because landscape urbanism developed an entirely new vocabulary that somehow a new design aesthetic would result! I initially dismissed landscape urbanism as the resurgence of post modernism with better graphics. In fact, landscape urbanism is the result of amazing technological advances in 3-D software. It is possible to create gravity-defying and sublime imagery in ways that I think Rich Haag would condemn as visual swindle.

Examples of landscape as urban infrastructure in the United States alone is prevalent; the emerald necklace in Boston is one example, Central Park and hundreds of urban golf courses and parks are other clear examples. It would be better to see urban landscapes as sustainable, expressive, and functional places wherever people chose to live. Keep it simple, make it ecologically based and sustainable, because once it's built and functioning no one could even consider removing it. Of course, this ecology would include all of the parts of the urban environment, and, if built right, would last for centuries rather than just decades.

One other very significant opportunity sprung from the desert. I began work on Paolo Soleri's most recent projects - Linear Cities; one sited in China and one sited conceptually. I remember well reading Soleri's books on arcologies, decades ago, and now I was immersed in this legendary view of how we will find meaning and efficiency in a nature-based morphology. I met with Soleri to hear more about his ideas and to see if I could be helpful with the continuation of his work. He left me with a gift from his garden—a persimmon, a beautiful and exotic fruit. I could imagine one day picking fresh fruit from the gardens of a linear city that I might one day help to build.

Even the beautiful sky of the desert, the naked mountains, peculiar flora and fauna, and restless weather could not distract me from the ankle of Phaedra. The groundwork is set to return to Seattle. Perhaps back to a rigorous and engaged design community. The freedom to reinvent myself in Arizona was a myth that just couldn't satisfy my thirst for making urban life meaningful. I hope my evolving perspective sets the table for a new and even more creative chapter of this journey.

I think the past might be less important now. The present and the prospect of an unknown future are more alluring than ever. Stephen Hawkins once described the universe in such poetic terms that I assumed his thought about perfection for myself. In essence, he said that the Big Bang, if it were perfect, would have ended in perfect balance. We, as living organisms, would not arise, if not for an anomaly, a ripple in the nearly perfect blast. Therefore, imperfection is the real creator and perfection is the goal. Yet perfection is unattainable because it would be stagnation.

This gives me great comfort, because I can think of no life more imperfect and out of balance than mine. It is also reassuring to realize that everything we are started billions of light years ago with the very first mistake…

"But the past, spread out ahead, dominates everything in sight."

—Zen and the Art of Motorcycle Maintenance by Alan Pirsig

THE JOURNEY BEGINS

The Visitor Centers at Mount St. Helens National Volcanic Monument

CASTLE ROCK, WASHINGTON, USA, 1997

While with EDAW, in collaboration with Spencer Associates and the USDA Forest Service
2005 National ASLA Design Honor Award

This project integrated two new visitor centers into the new landscape formed by Mount St. Helen's 1980 eruption. Enormous parking lots, buildings, and site features are placed in a manner to evoke an emotional response from the drama of the landscape. The forms given to these features are poetic gestures - an arrow through a crescent-shaped parking lot for Coldwater Ridge Visitor Center and the profile of a resting butterfly for the parking lot of the Johnston Ridge Observatory.

Artifacts from the volcanic eruption blast artifacts were preserved, or catalogued, stored and reinstalled to elevate or make "super real" the level of landscape devastation. The message of the eruption and its aftermath are prevalent in these details and are exemplified in the fractured colored concrete paving, the light poles that are colored to match the nearby flora, and remaining tree stumps. The path leading to Johnston Ridge is a dramatic journey that takes you towards the volcano at a barely visible, but perceivable slope. This journey ends with a view into a breathtaking valley two thousand feet below.

Coldwater Ridge Visitor Center was completed in 1993 and Johnston Ridge Observatory was completed in 1997.

Above: Viewing Mount St. Helens from the platform
Below: View of Mount St. Helens eruption in 2005
Facing: Light fixtures were designed to create a minimal profile against the sky and Earth colors were chosen to complement the landscape

MOUNT ST. HELENS
NATIONAL VOLCANIC MONUMENT
COLDWATER RIDGE
VISITOR CENTER

Above: The Coldwater Ridge Visitor Center complements the landscape
Below: Sketch of path at Coldwater Visitor Center

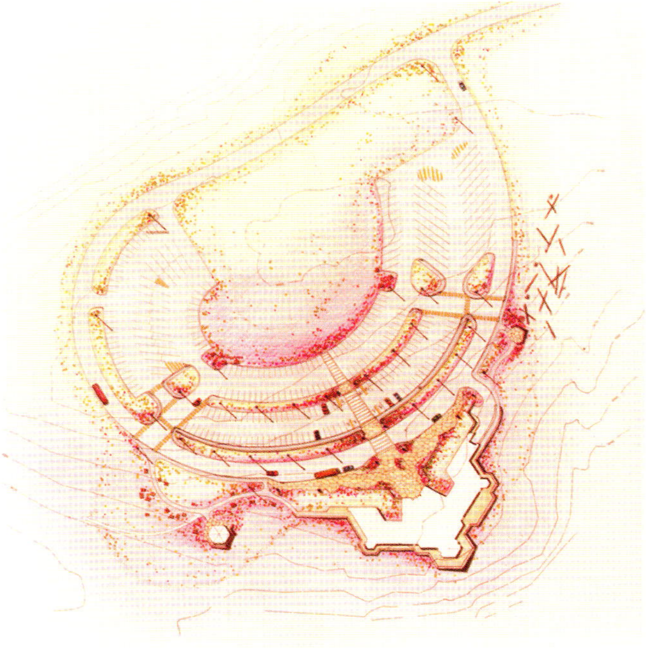

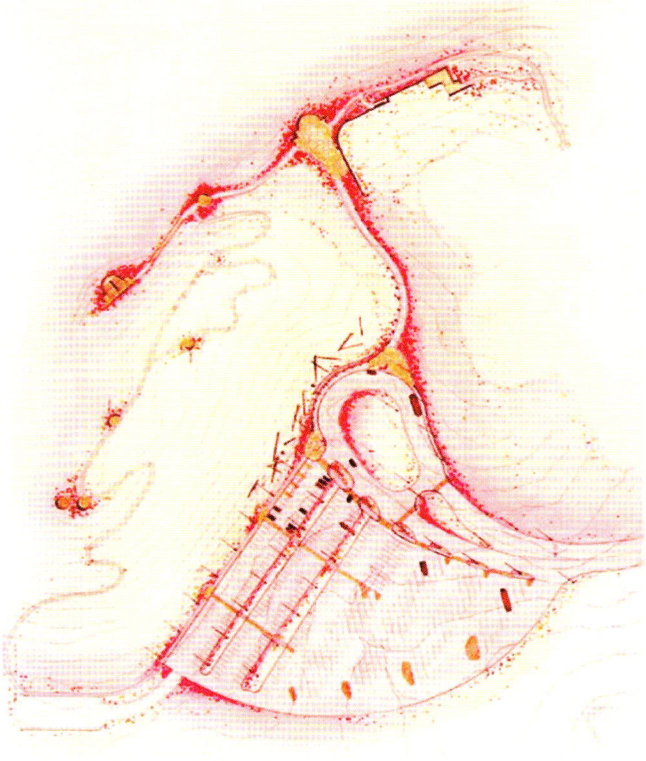

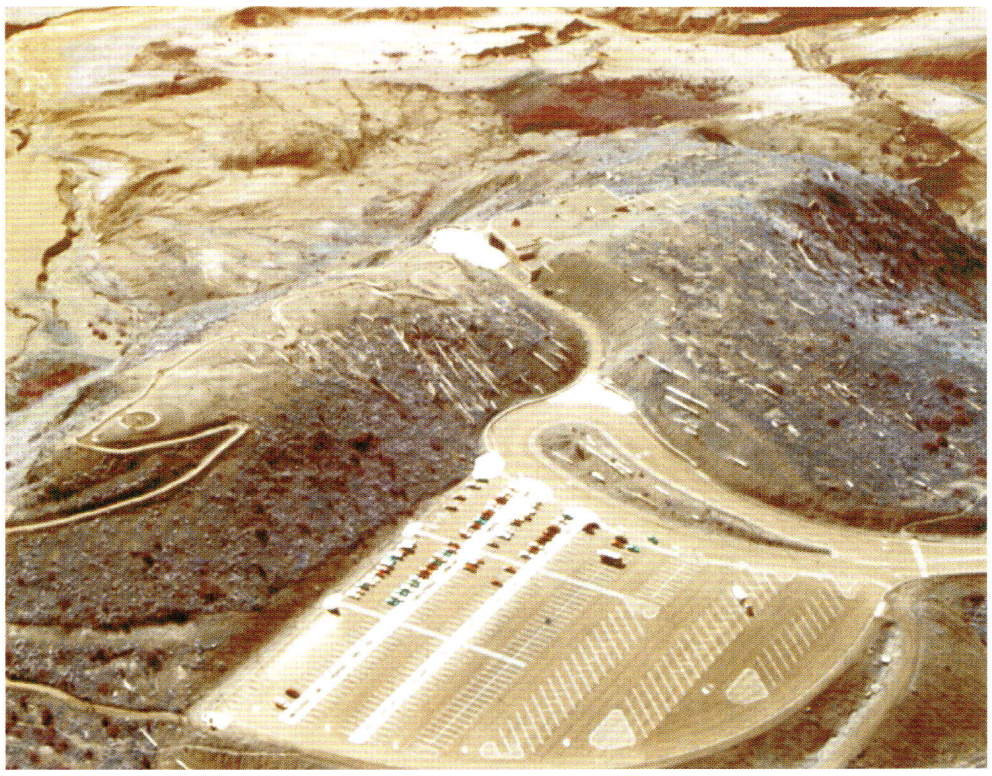

Above left: Coldwater Visitor Center plan
Above right: Aerial view of the visitor center
Below left: Johnston Ridge Observatory plan
Below right: Aerial view of the Ridge

The volcano erupted with great fury on a day when I was in studio at Washington State Universtiy. It blotted out the sun and threatened to end the term four weeks early. Eight years later, I would find myself on the design team to bring people back to see the event aftermath and recovery. I could not think of a more humbling experience than to work with an active volcano, like Turrell and his volcano, and to see it as the ultimate earthworks. I did not want to take away anything from the site or compete with it but instead complement it. I did not want the visitors to be "comfortable" in the presence of such power. Here I learned restraint and appreciation for nature's process.

—Charles Anderson

Facing: View of volcano from Johnston Ridge Observatory
Above: View of parking lot at Johnston Ridge Observatory
Below: Path at Coldwater Visitor Center

Facing above: Overview of Johnston Ridge Observatory and platform
Facing below: The entrance to Coldwater Ridge Visitor Center
Below: Viewing platform from the observatory
Bottom: The 2005 eruption of Mount St. Helens from Spirit Lake

The Arthur Ross Terrace at the American Museum of Natural History

NEW YORK, NEW YORK, USA, 2000

In collaboration with Kathryn Gustafson and Polshek Partnership Architects
2003 National ASLA Design Merit Award

The Arthur Ross terrace was part of the New Hayden Planetarium project and an invited design competition that required the retrofitting of a project already under construction. This rooftop terrace is designed to be a stage set for the study of astronomy and Earth's natural history. Wedge-shaped planetary shadows from the sphere of Hayden Planetarium are expressed through paving across the plaza to the doorstep of the historic museum. The darkest, central portion of the plaza playfully depicts the Orion star cluster with tiny mirrors and fiber-optic lights. Water jets and cut granite "meteor-trail" rills add a playful aspect to this Celestial garden. The forms and plantings of the plaza enhance the garden. Sky blue flowers, Ginkgo trees harkening back to the carboniferous period, and a mostly native plant palette connect ing the terrace to its living plant history.

Alcoves with large, flat benches along one side of the plaza provide seating and create impromptu classrooms for the many school children who visit the planetarium. Dancing water jets serve to cool the terrace and children on hot summer days, while at night the blue colors emanating from the new planetarium building reflect dramatically across the wet dark granite.

This project needed a new face put on the bones and structure of a project previously designed and under construction. New York City requires tough trees and nothing is tougher than the ancient Ginkgo tree. That tree reaches back into the history of life on this planet and the Planetarium looks back into the history of the stars.

—Charles Anderson

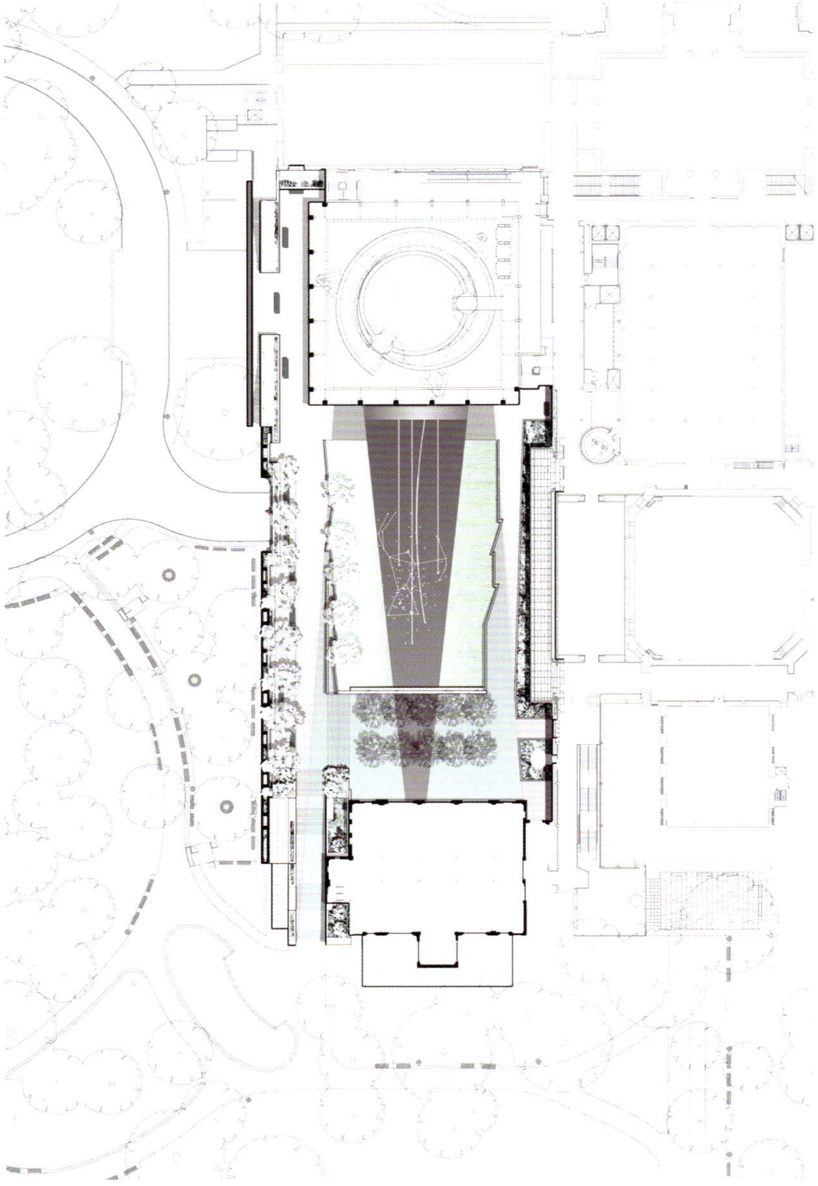

Above: Terrace illustrative plan
Facing: View of terrace at night with planetarium in the background

Above: View of the terrace with the ginkgo grove behind
Facing clockwise: Detail of adjustable water jet; Detail of rough cast aluminum tree grates; View across the terrace to the Planetarium

Facing above: View of terrace in the daytime
Facing below: View of terrace at night
Above: Dancing water jets represent asteroids streaking through the constellation Orion
Right: The water jets are a respite from summer heat

Above: Long view of the promenade
Facing: View of "learning benches" and the "astronomy wall" to the left

Satsop Development Park

ELMA, WASHINGTON, USA, 2000

In collaboration with Collins Woerman Architecture
2005 WASLA Design Honor Award for Works in Progress

The design team worked with Grays Harbor Planning Development Authority to prepare a master plan to guide the transformation of a defunct nuclear power generation plant into a high-tech industrial technology park. The design for the cooling tower park incorporates the cooling towers of the partially completed Satsop power project. One of the towers is transformed into a park and stands as a giant oculus to the sky. This setting provides the opportunity to fly a kite, to watch birds ride the air currents and the updrafts, to hear the echo of the chamber, or to just marvel at the sheer immensity of the plant's dimensions.

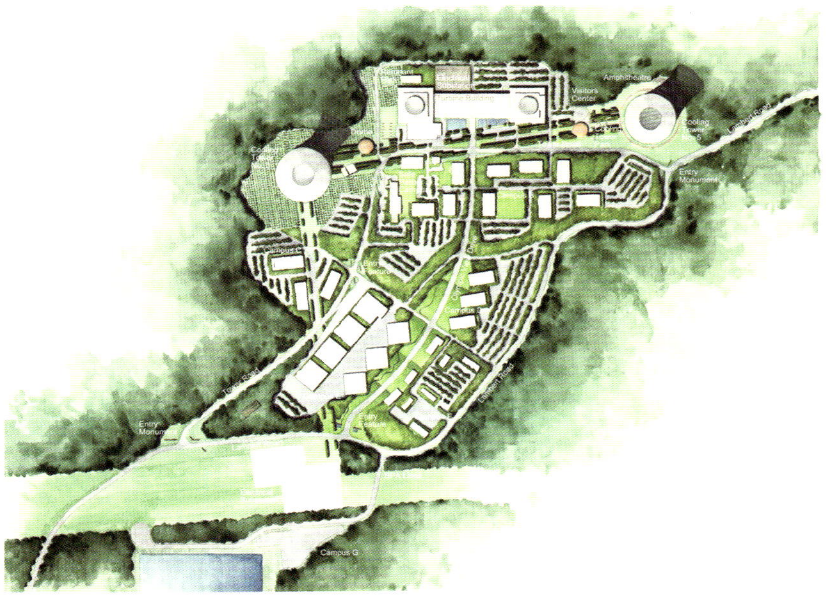

Above: 2020 Master plan
Below: Proposed view of elevation platform inside the cooling tower
Facing: Interior view of the cooling tower

Above: The cooling tower's dynamic character
Right: The enormous scale of the 496-foot cooling tower

The great cooling towers stood up over the canopy of second and third growth timber. The two together made a kind of poetry, especially now that the nuclear components have no function. My primary goals were the preservation of the towers as a sort of modern Gothic cathedral, growing a native plant arboretum, and creating the right tension between the incompatible worlds of industry and nature. These towers stand in a hostile natural world, the story of a nuclear folly forever told.

—Charles Anderson

Image: Size comparison with Space Needle

Facing above and above: Aerial view of the park

Trillium Projects

SEATTLE DEPARTMENT OF PARKS AND RECREATION, SEATTLE, WASHINGTON, USA, 2000

Six sites located in Seattle, Washington: Seward Park Native Plant Garden, Genesee Meadow, Pritchard Beach Wetland Parks, Colman Park, Roxhill Bog, and 500 Area Discovery Park
2004 ASLA Design Merit Award

The Trillium Projects acknowledge beauty and design, but take the science of "urban nature" very seriously. The projects question the notion of urban restoration where designers define ecologies as separate from human activities: the artifice that is our city is inspiration for artful landscape expressions. By understanding that native plants behave differently within an urban context, new sustainable plant communities emerge, creating plant and wildlife diversity that is beneficial for the environment and people. As native plants require fewer resources to construct and maintain these landscapes, the Trillium Projects are not only designs with nature but are designs for nature. There are numerous co-conspirators for these projects, from Seattle schools using the sites as outdoor classrooms for environmental education, to volunteer contributing thousands of hours, to public and private agencies and companies. The Trillium projects speak of community, where plants, wildlife inhabit, and people grow together.

In implementing these projects, Charles Anderson has been working closely with the Starflower Foundation, an organization promoting native landscapes as scientific and cultural resources, and with the City of Seattle. Due to the success of these parks, the City of Seattle is expected to continue to develop the Trillium Projects for future explorers and strollers.

A decade and a half ago a very passionate client began a search to find someone who was interested in the re-establishment of native plants in the city. Fortunately for me that became the start of a very long-term urban ecological experiment, including over 20 projects, the biggest of these were the Trillium Projects. Ann Lennarz and her Starflower Foundation supplied millions of native plants to open spaces throughout Seattle and we had something to do with almost all of their placement. It's about more than plants, however, it's about the bugs and bunnies that look for them and the people who learn from these places about our connection to nature, even in the city.

—Charles Anderson

Images above: Scenes from the Trillium Projects
From top: Colman Park, Gennessee Meadow, Seward Park, Pritchard Wetland Park

GARDEN/OLD GROWTH FOREST:
Seward Park Native Plant Garden

The Native Plant Garden at Seward Park, comprised of regional native plants, welcomes visitors to Seward Park via the garden and a newly restored environmental education center. Seward Park is one of three intact old growth forests in the metro region; trees in this park exceed 200 feet in height. Appropriately, this garden was also the first Seattle Department of Parks and Recreation project to use an all-native plant palette. As the park visitor begins the journey, the first of four interpretive signs explains sensory information about natural history and ethno-botany that is later experienced on walks through the forest.

Initially 250 square feet, this native plant garden successfully grew to an acre and soon became the home for the Audubon Nature Center. Starting a garden in the shadows of an old growth forest seems trivial, but it wasn't about the big trees only, instead, it was also the story of the trillium and the ant. The sticky seeds of the flower affix to the ants that arrive looking for food. When they return home, the other ants remove the seed and inadvertently plant it. We planted trillium and other plants to tell these stories to generations to come, to see how we are all part of the stories of nature - even an urban nature.

—Charles Anderson

Above: Fallen Madrona tree as a landscape feature
Below left: Illustrative site plan
Below right: The accessible pathway through the native plant garden leads to the old growth forest of the Seward Park
Facing: View of a bigleaf maple in the "Magnificent Forest"

MEADOW:
Genesee Meadow

First a bay of Lake Washington, then a landfill, now this 15-acre portion of Genesee Park is a restored wildflower meadow. Trails meander around mounded woodland islands, grasslands, and wildflowers, all reclaiming the site for habitat. Interpretive signs describe the site's native plant communities, wildlife habitat and historical uses. Three large earth mounds allow trees and shrubs to colonize the meadow landscape and vastly improve nesting and foraging habitat. The Audubon Society monitors bird populations on the site, and the Washington Native Plant Society observes the process of plant succession on the landfill. The soil used to build these mounds is from a series of landslides, a natural process of the Puget basin.

The former landfill site was settling and the vast landscape of mowed grasses was getting harder and harder to maintain. We lopped off five of the fifteen acres of turf and turned it into a meadow - the first in the city. The birders went crazy with the new found habitat, and the savanna sparrow finally had a place to live in the city.

—Charles Anderson

Above: Illustrative Site Plan
Below left: Lupine flowering in the meadow
Below right: Dormant grasses in summer
Facing: Reused railroad timbers demarcate the meadow perimeter

WETLAND:
Pritchard Beach Wetland Park

Through the synthesis of ecology and art, twelve acres that were once the lake bed of Lake Washington, and more recently abandoned storage flats and soggy turf, have been restored into a contemplative ecological classroom of scrub-shrub lowland and upland forest. Boardwalks and trails are carefully integrated with the planting design to direct views and circulation through discrete landscape features such as the Alder Gallery, the Willow Circle, and the Apple Crescent, while limiting disturbance to the delicate landscape. At the heart of the project a new pond connects to Lake Washington via a seasonal stream. Wetlands of all types are featured - from lake to wet meadow, forested wetland, and open water pond. Each type serves as a classroom and exemplifies the diversity of ecological types that just a few acres can provide.

At the heart of this park we dug a new pond and planted an alder forest around it. When we were asked, "Why more water when so close to the lake?", the answer was simple. Big water is good for some wildlife and small water is good for much more. We scooped out the soil to make a mound for an amphitheater, to look out over the pond. Inside the mound we entombed invasive non-native plants. Without the pond, the diversity of the plants and animals wouldn't come to this site - nor would the people to enjoy them.

—Charles Anderson

Above: Landscape plan, highlighting various poetic places like "Willow Circle", "Alder Gallery" and "Maple Cathedral"
Below left: Pond with hogwire fence. The fence is invisible today. It was installed to meet park safety standards, and is buried in a thicket of wild rose
Below Right: Box of Rocks amphitheater, a place for small gatherings to learn about the different types of wetlands
Facing above: View of the constructed pond. The water level fluctuates with the levels of nearby Lake Washington
Facing below: Edge between the wetland meadows and mown turf

SHORELINE:
Colman Park

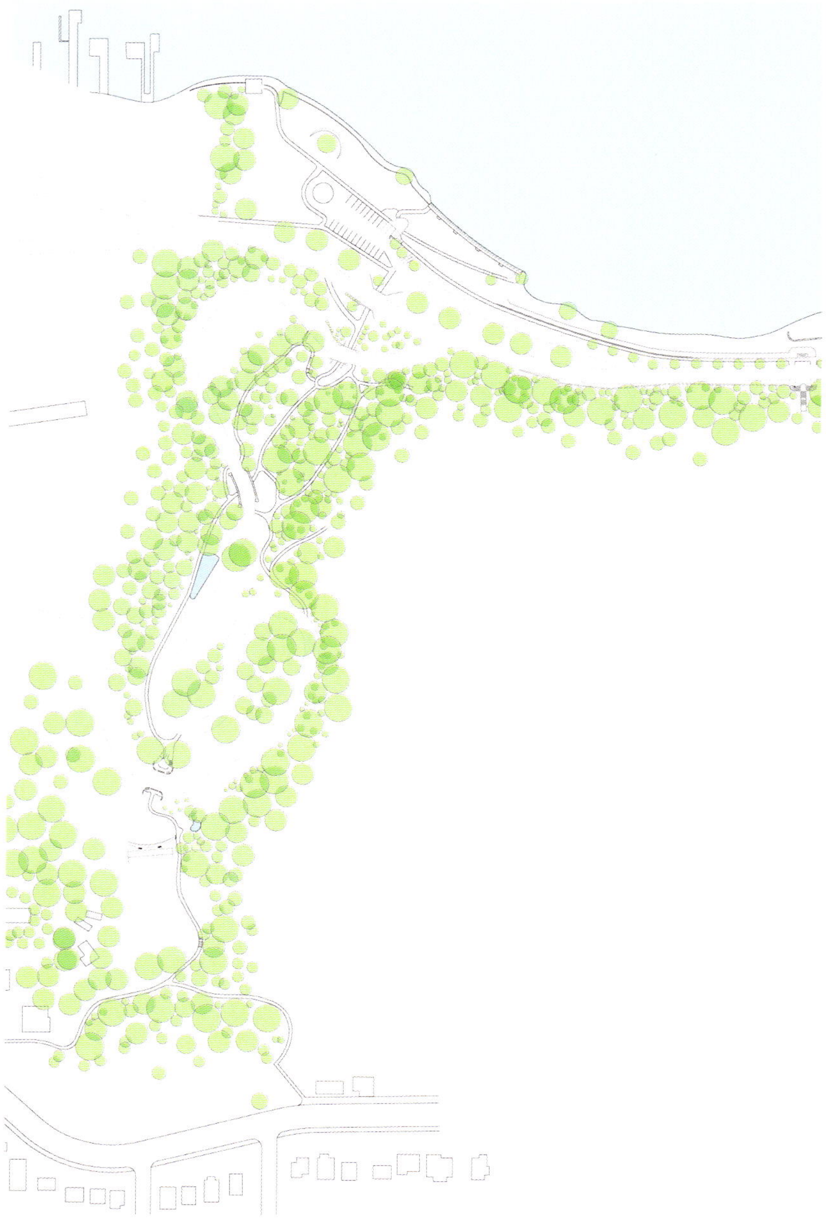

Colman Park, originally planned by the Olmsted Brothers, is rich with historical significance. The current design is structured to complement historic aspects of the park, while restoring and enhancing wildlife habitat. Interpretive signs describe both the cultural and ecological importance of the park, explaining both the Olmsted legacy and shoreline with its riparian and upland forest native plant communities. Along Lake Washington, a successful low-tech method for creating a sustainable shoreline was implemented. One of the restoration tactics used included the protection of the shoreline except in select locations where non-native willows have clung vicariously to an eroding shoreline. All the willows will eventually fall into Lake Washington. One willow that fell became the local "Starbucks" for aquatic animals, and the walkway overlooking the tree is now a great spot to observe turtles, water fowl and muskrats.

An Olmsted brothers park needed help. Funds for maintenance had dwindled for over a decade. We brought both cultural restoration and habitat to the park. When a large "non-native" tree fell into the lake, we left it to entropy. It instantly became a magnet for wildlife. Ducks, turtles, cormorants, and many more species vie for a place, only to scatter at the site of an eagle overhead.

—Charles Anderson

Above: Illustrative Site Plan for improvements to this Olmsted Park
Left and facing right: Wildlife enjoying a place to perch out of the water. This is the "Starbucks" of Lake Washington
Facing above: Shoreline of Colman Park

Facing: Shoreline of Colman Park
Above: View of rain garden

BOG:
Roxhill Bog

At Roxhill Bog an ecological system unique to an urban setting was created. The community-initiated planting of 200,000 native plants aided in restoring natural systems and habitat to create a unique educational resource. Roxhill Bog is a remnant bog and wetland, which was uncovered and shaped into a grid pattern reminiscent of the historical agricultural use of bogs in this area. Situated at the headwaters of Longfellow Creek, the project plays an important role in improving water quality, managing water flow into Longfellow Creek, and supporting downstream salmon habitat restoration. Water is detained on site in a subterranean basin below a new playing field which was created from the fill that once covered the bog. The flow from the basin is metered to extend the available water supply during the dry season.

It wasn't the restoration of a remnant bog that interested me as much as it was the possibility of a new kind of urban ecology, one fashioned in a structured way that would evolve into an unclassified urban wetland. The runoff from adjacent lands, ball fields, streets and backyards, riff with anything that affects this place.

—Charles Anderson

Above: Master plan
Below left: Community work party to plant the pond
Below right: Community art project of white wire frames in the bog
Facing above: Aerial view showing the gridded pathways reminiscent of the old blueberry fields
Below left on the facing page: Constructed wetland meadow in the summer
Below right on the facing page: Redwing blackbird visiting the constructed pond

FOREST:
500 Area Discovery Park

Restoration of the 500 Area involved the demolition of 24 Army barracks, as well as a plan for restoring native woodlands and integrating the site with the overall Discovery Park Master Plan developed by Dan Kiley in 1974. Groves of white-trunked birch and aspen trees define the footprints of the demolished barracks, thereby acting as ghosts or memories of the white-clad barrack buildings. Alder, a robust native early successional species, was planted throughout the site to establish the initial forest cover. Over time, the alders will fix nitrogen and prepare the soil for the giant conifers of the restored native forest.

The soon-to-be demolished white-painted barracks were impossible to ignore, especially because each building came with numerous stories from its former occupants. The footprints of each of these buildings became an emblematic native plant nursery, featuring white trunked birch and aspen trees. As long as one of these trees survives in this new forest, the ghost of this former life remains.

—Charles Anderson

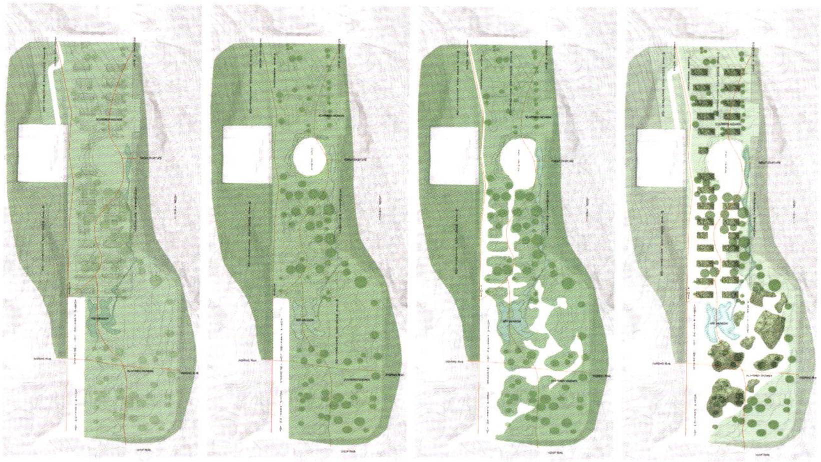

Top: A view showing the contrast between the existing trees and the "barrack" native plant nurseries
Above: Plans illustrating the growth of the forest over a twenty-year period
Below: A composite image of the regraded site of the "Skyspace"
Facing: Aerial view showing the "barrack" footprints and the crescent-shaped "Skyspace". Invasive plants were entombed in the mounds

Hill House

SEATTLE, WASHINGTON, USA, 2003

In collaboration with Tom Kundig, Olson Kundig Architects

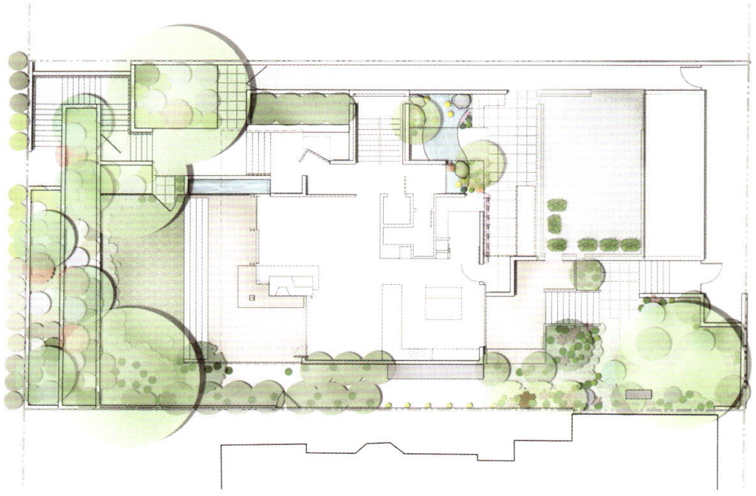

Perched on Queen Anne Hill, this home features native plants such as Big Leaf and Vine Maples, Salal, Snowberry, Tall Oregon Grape, Bunchberry, Western Trillium. Because of the urban setting and limited space, areas not normally considered for plants provide landscape opportunities. Nursery areas on the roof and backyard will accommodate young plants to be used for restoration efforts in other parks. Spaces under ramps are filled with ferns and mosses. The passage between the garage and back door become a verdant wetland. A metal grating walkway spans the water feature below which is filled with Giant Horsetail, Skunk Cabbage, and Slough Sedge.

The project is tailored to the owners, who are constantly tending and revising the landscape as they learn how the garden is recolonized by native plants. It's a garden that borrows the views of Puget Sound and the habitat of neighboring big trees, serving as a much needed wildlife refuge in the city.

Above: Illustrative site plan
Below: Boulders and ladders for access were incorporated into the "sun gardens"
Facing: The house sits high on the site to capture views and light. The retaining walls are bedrock for the gardens - to be colonized by the sun-loving native palnts

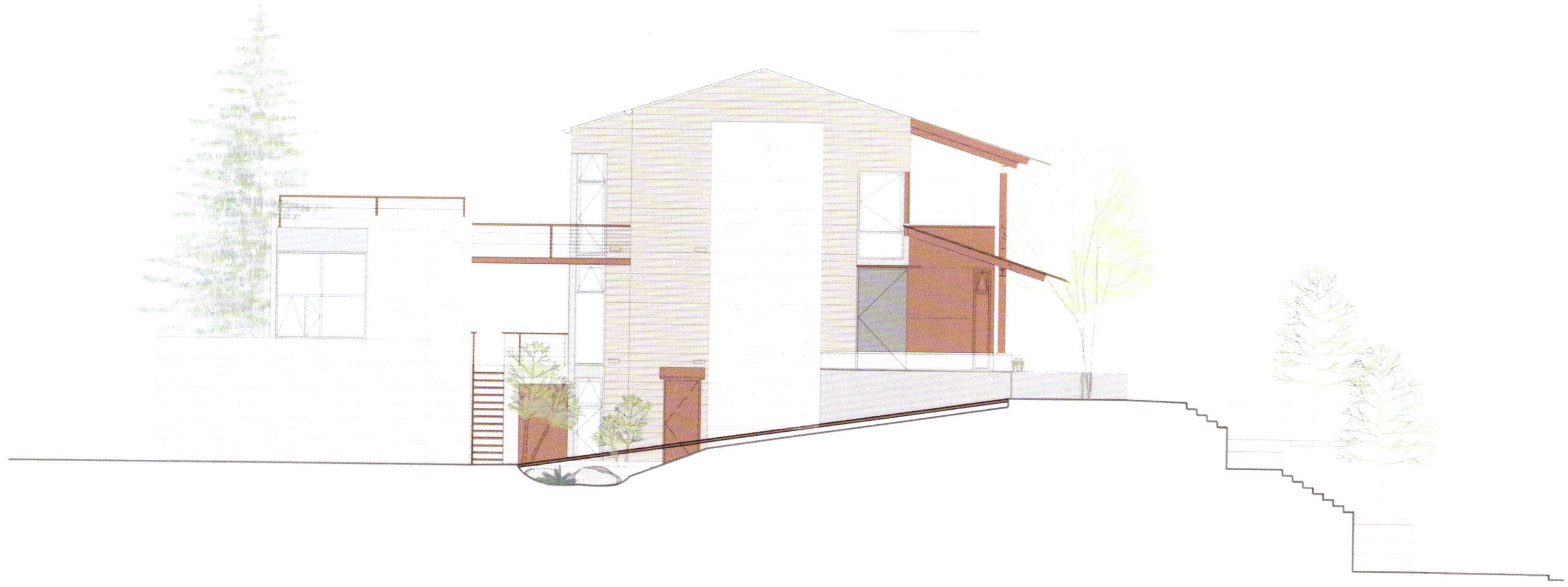

Architect Tom Kundig's houses grow right out of the earth. They even rust. They are works in progress, like the gardens. This is an all-native plant project with a great variety of plants in a very small space. It's a garden of prospect and refuge.

—Charles Anderson

Above: A cross section illustrating the profile of the site
Right: Window opens up to outdoor gardens
Facing: Native plants colonizing the sun garden

Facing above: Water garden grotto
Facing below: Old logs were added to the garden to nourish the soil and provide habitat
Above: Water garden at the entrance
Right: Native planting at upper terrace

Facing: Grotto garden with bridge to garage roof garden
Above: Water garden grotto showing metal stairs and walkways
Right: Roof garden over garage

Beijing 2008 Olympics Competition

BEIJING, CHINA, 2003

Finalist for Invited Competition
In collaboration with XWHO Design and Richard Haag

The organizers of the Beijing Olympics sought designs through a competition for the grounds of the event, China's first opportunity to host. This design was based on the notion of a landscape sequence of from "Birth Space" and ending with the "Future Space". The team discussed the intersections between the Eastern understanding of this sequence with the Western, and the design thematically reflects human emotions and a spirit of cooperation and competition. The main entry gate is a colossal Olympic symbol, materially borrowing from the nearby Birdsnest Stadium and its alignment with the series of gates which emanate on axis from the Forbidden City of central Beijing.

China was even bigger than I imagined. For some reason it felt like I had been there before, the earth seemed familiar and the culture, somehow familiar too, maybe because I could see my culture more clearly from being here. Rich Haag and I were holed up in a conference room trying to connect a Western design philosophy with our counterparts of Xia and Xia's office. There was a curious love of nature in this country but not quite the "nature", the wilds, that I had grown to understand. Nature here seemed to be green and healthful, not necessarily ecological. Ying Yang became clearer than ever to me - the power of opposites to coexist and make each stronger, especially in the composition of a design.

—Charles Anderson

Below: Proposed entry gate to the Olympics with the main stadium in the background
Facing above: Haag's idea for a "cathederal of trees"
Facing below: A sequence illustrating the four seasons

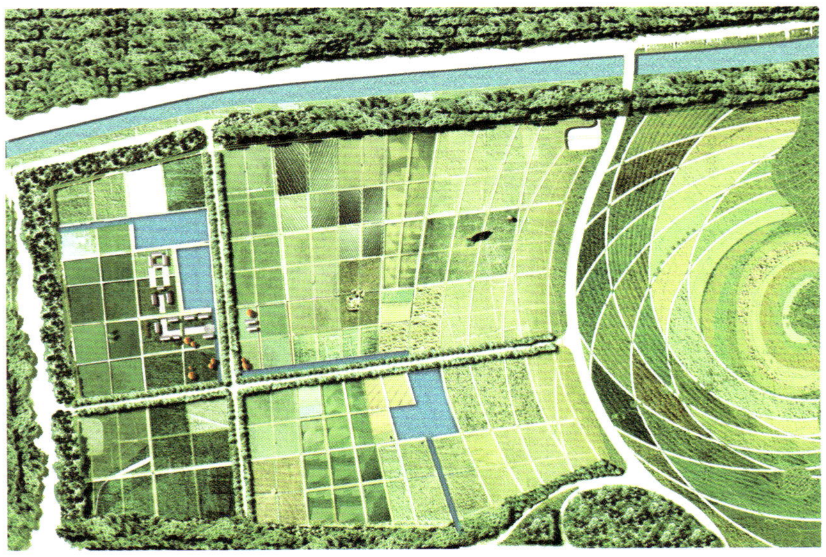

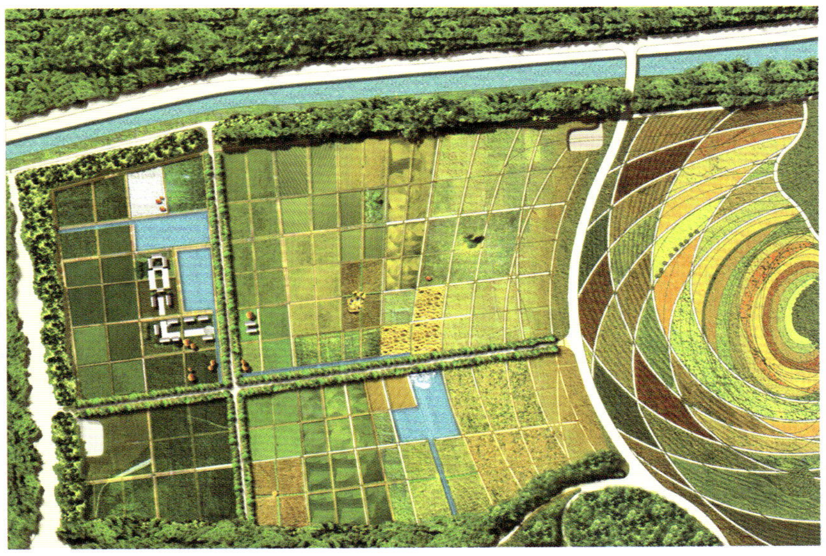

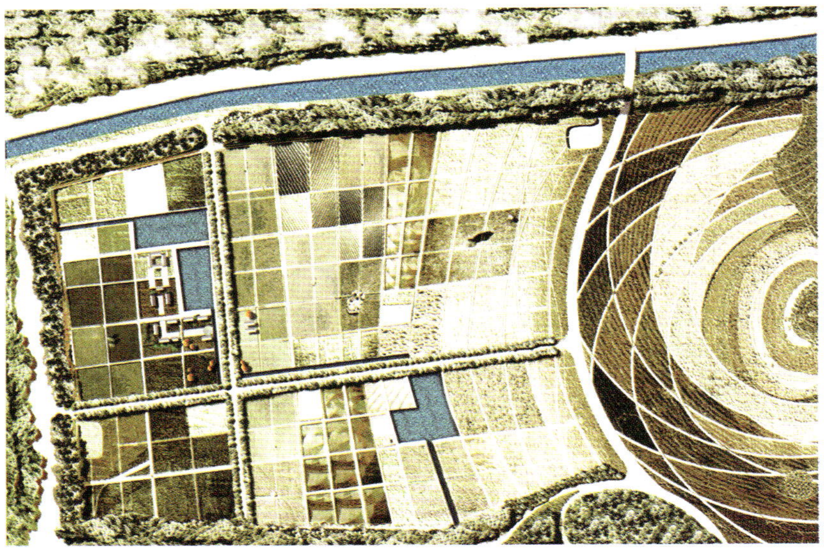

Kingdoms of Discovery

DALIAN, CHINA, 2003

Landscapes have the power to connect, enhance, define and accentuate. The setting for this theme park is at Golden Pebble Beach, one of north China's preeminent vacation destinations for its growing middle class. The landscape plan for the Kingdoms of Discovery theme park in Dalian provides a strong definition of the park's boundaries while creating distinct places of beauty within its shell and around an ocean-fed lake. Through the careful selection and arrangement of plantings, visitors are offered a variety of experiences that reinforce the themes of the various areas while maintaining a consistent atmosphere of pleasure and enjoyment. The design of the planting areas is complimented by bold paving designs that further enhance the visitor's experience and define the unique character of each themed zone. The project was completed in 2005.

On a cold winter day we walked around the site to discuss our plans with the local landscape contractor. We explained our ideas, we talked about plants and paving and water features. I was given a World War II issue coat to keep me warm. I was joined by over a dozen people and felt like a military commander. They brought thousands of enormous trees to plant in the very early spring - it took a small army to plant them in the grid that I had asked for.

—Charles Anderson

Above: Master site plan
Below: Some of the over five thousand large trees used for the project
Facing above: Aerial view of the park
Facing below: The fire platform over the lake

Waterfront Place

RENO, NEVADA, USA, 2004

In collaboration with Carlos Zapata Studio (unbuilt)

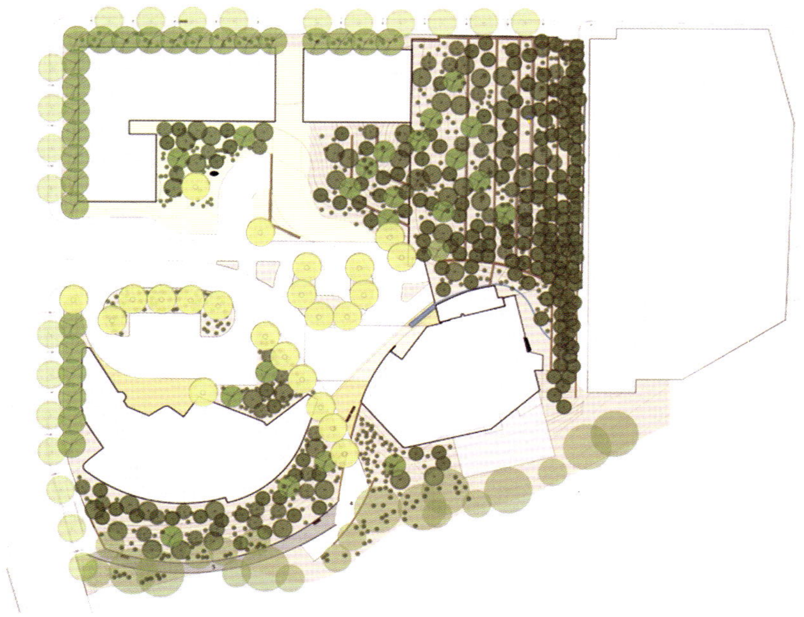

This last open city block in the heart of Reno provides the opportunity to redefine the city's relationship with the Truckee River. The design for the 3.5 acre site seeks to create a new waterfront district that integrates the natural feel of the river with a modern hotel, residential tower and art studios. Inspired by not only the river but also the geology of the mountains, the design incorporates shifting geologic fault lines and horizontal stratifications of the Nevada landscape. An 18-story "tree wall" rises from the river to conceal a nearby parking garage and complete the metaphor.

An elegant glass condo, hotel and arts center was part of a plan to bring signature design to Reno. Native plants were an integral part of the landscape. The plant communities rose eighteen stories on terraces. We called it a "treescraper", and it mainly functioned as a suitable complement to the sleek new tower, but also screened an adjacent park structure. The trees and plants of the nearby mountains will inhabit this urban ecology.

—Charles Anderson

Above: Illustrative site plan
Below: Section showing the relationship of the "treescraper" to the skyscraper
Facing above: View of tower and streetscape
Facing below: Aerial view of proposed tower and landscape

2nd Street

Madison Art House

SEATTLE, WASHINGTON, USA, 2005

In collaboration with Roy McMakin/Domestic Architecture

This 1.5-acre site overlooking Lake Washington is heavily wooded and historically significant. The project features landscape rooms and places, including the Nostalgia Garden, the Red House Patio, the Hollow, Belvedere and the Big Woods. These places entice future artists to create site-specific installations or inspire the owners to find artworks. The different elevations of these rooms and the high, hill-home capture distant views to Mt. Rainier and the Cascades. Conversely, intimate inward-looking rooms are places of refuge. Native plants are a major component of these gardens, except for preserved existing trees, specimens, and the rose and ornamental filled Nostalgia Garden.

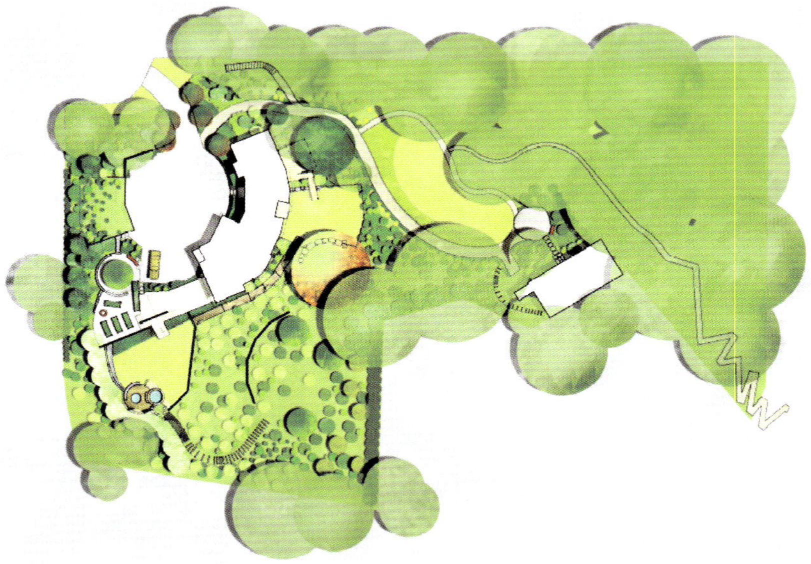

Above: Final landscape site plan
Below: Auto-court with recycled concrete paving
Facing: Edible garden with iconic apple tree

Working with an artist who also served as the architect presented its own surprising challenges. This house is certainly unexpected, employing a domestic vernacular on a very grand scale. The landscape became a playful collage of my minimalist approach and the artist's penchant for folly. It reflected precisely the nature of the inhabitants.

—Charles Anderson

Above: View of entry drive to auto-court
Facing: View of building from auto-court

Facing: View of the deck from backyard
Above: Outdoor dining court step to grass terrace

Above: Belvedere grass terrace
Right: Belvedere area with preserved Japanese Maple
Facing: View of nostalgia garden with red house in the distance

Facing: Hot tub with view of Lake Washington
Above: Belvedere grass terrace with hot tub

Above: View of the Nostalgia Garden

Above: Stabilized gravel path to the Red House

Image: Nostalgia Garden with Red House

Tables of Water

SEATTLE, WASHINGTON, USA, 2005

In collaboration with Jim Olson, Olson Kundig Architects
2006 ASLA National Design Honor Award

Seeking to engage a relationship between landscape, art and architecture, the minimalist design of this 3.5-acre residence extends the walls of the house to the outside, creating rooms, framing views and making space for sculpture. Elements of water are carried through the site, at first only seen, then heard, as water features and finally as a tactile experience, for swimming. Two less formal gardens break down the structured geometry of evergreen hedges and bosques. The Garden of the Wilds highlights palms, responding to the existing tropical plants around the site. The Moon Garden's night blooming plants and perennials offer a quiet place to wander, particularly in the evening.

Above: Illustrative master site plan
Below: View over tables of water to Lake Washington
Facing: Cut-leaf Japanese maples flank the view through the dining room to the lake

Above: View across terrace and swimming pool
Below: A Chihuly sculpture rests on the terrace beside the infinity-edged pool
Facing: Detail of tables of water

This existing estate came complete with an extraordinary collection of large and rare plants. The problem was that most of them had to be moved to make way for a new residence. The architect and the client loved Mies van der Rohe's Barcelona Pavilion - a very different place. Here we organized the gardens into deliberate groups around a very minimalist parti. The pool, spa and water feature complete the landscape design, as minimal as possible, as "tables of water" at times difficult to distinguish from the adjacent surfaces.

—Charles Anderson

Image: The living room of the outdoor garden

Above: Hot tub with infinity edges
Below: Detail of tables of water
Facing above: Close-up of Chihuly sculpture
Two images below on the facing page: Curved paths at Moon Garden

Facing above: View of the tropical garden
Facing below left: Entry driveway
Facing below right: View of the lakeside terrace
Above: Night view of the "tables of water"
Right: Chihuly sculpture at night

Gardens of the Olympic Sculpture Park

SEATTLE ART MUSEUM, SEATTLE, WASHINGTON, USA, 2007

In collaboration with Weiss / Manfredi Architects
2008 AIA Honor Award
2007 National ASLA Design Honor Award
2005 Selected for "Groundswell, Constructing the Contemporary Landscape" Exhibition, The Museum of Modern Art, NY
2005 Seattle Design Commission + Mayor's Commendation Award

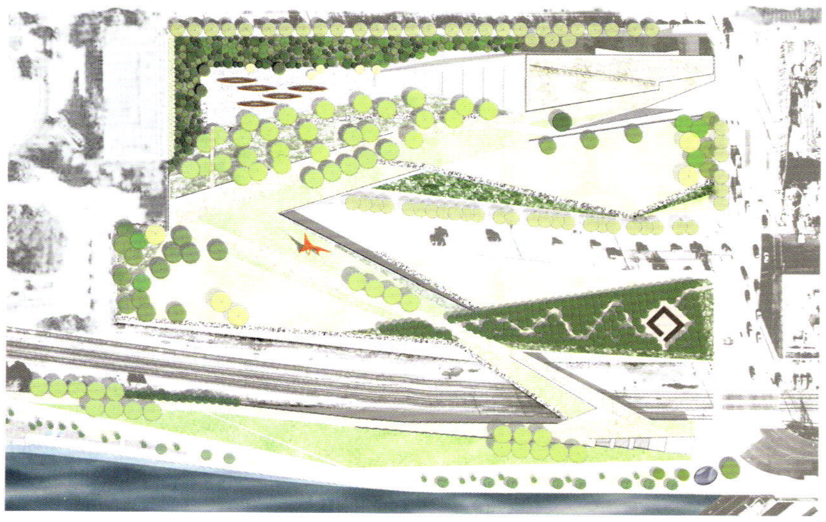

Above: Master plan
Below: Calder "Eagle" with Olympic Mountains in the distance
Facing: Aerial view of Olympic Sculpture Park

The Gardens of the Olympic Sculpture Park are the clothing that dresses the land of an abandoned fuel storage site. A reversed Z-shaped central path traverses roads and railroad tracks, as it connects the urban core of the city to the vast landscape of Puget Sound and its namesake, the Olympic Mountains. These connections are also reflected in a series of gardens, all distinctive prototypical landscapes of a "mountain to shore" narrative: The Valley, The Greensward, The Grove, The Meadows, The Shore, and The Tides. The settings are landscapes for sculpture, from large works to subtle time-based pieces. The relationship of sculpture, landscape and architecture are composed with a renewed enthusiasm.

The Valley stretches back to prehistoric times and pre-European contact to the region. It predates written language and represents the fascination we have with our past. Adjacent to the pavilion, this is the beginning of a mountain-to-shore narrative of the Northwest landscape. The Grove is a contemporary garden which respectfully questions control over nature by enlisting an unruly tree, Quaking Aspen, into a grid. It is a triangular-shaped forest with rooms cut into it for sculpture. The Meadows accommodate changing uses, including future earthworks and other art installations. It is open space that has the seasonal excitement of wildflowers in striking contrast to the turf grass areas and forested portions of the park. The Shore is, in many ways, a place where we respect our everchanging lives, predictable tides, and the unknown universe of the seas. The saltwater shoreline is one of the mildest (although not warmest) climatic zones of the Pacific Northwest. Shifting sand, grasses and salt-tolerant plants dress this sun-soaked landscape. The Tides features kelp, algae and other intertidal zone plants that are revealed and concealed with the changing tides. The sounds of a thriving industrial marine environment and its complement, restored marine habitat, offer the only place where people and the waters of the Pacific can meet in downtown Seattle. The interstitial spaces between these gardens are landscapes of grass and meadows. The lawn, or Greensward, parallels the Z-path and becomes a sixth precinct for sculpture and other pedestrian-oriented activities. This is an iconic composition of seating areas and shade trees that speaks to our universal view of a park.

The settings created by these landscapes will elicit responses from artists, who will produce content for the park, from large works to subtle time-based pieces. The gardens address the everchanging views of the role of a park in the city and art in the landscape. Through these layers of meaning and process, a new paradigm of park has emerged.

Left: A view of the grove, meadows, and valley

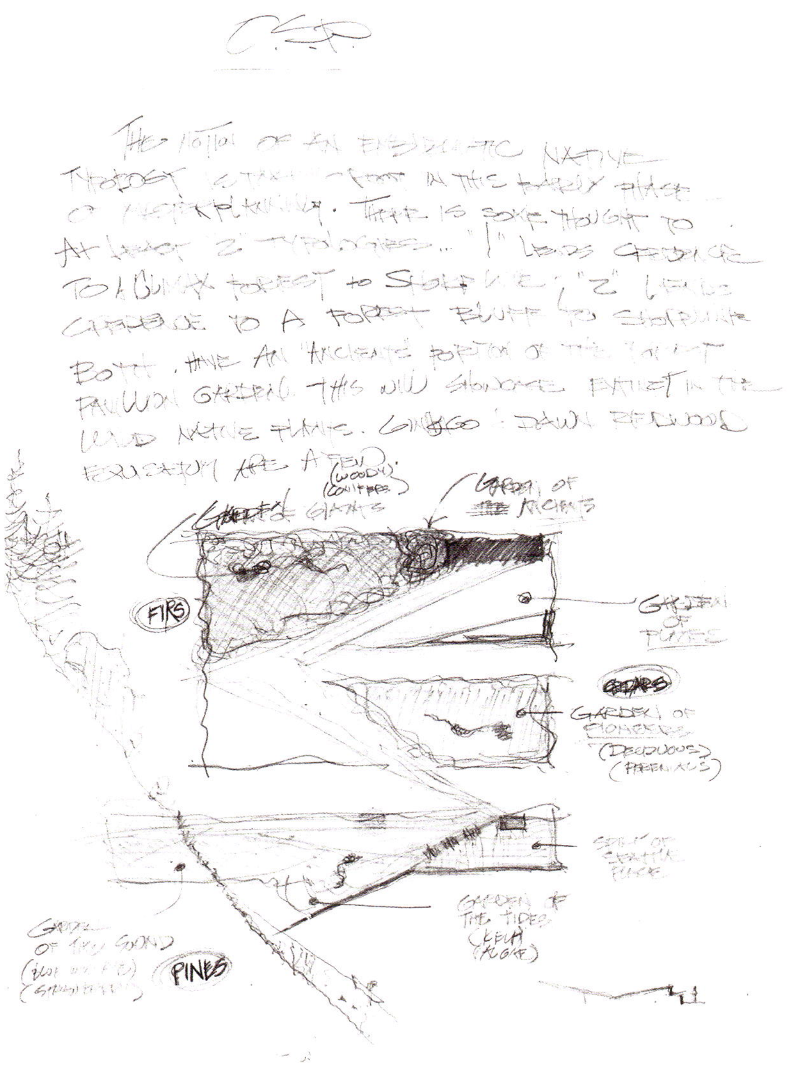

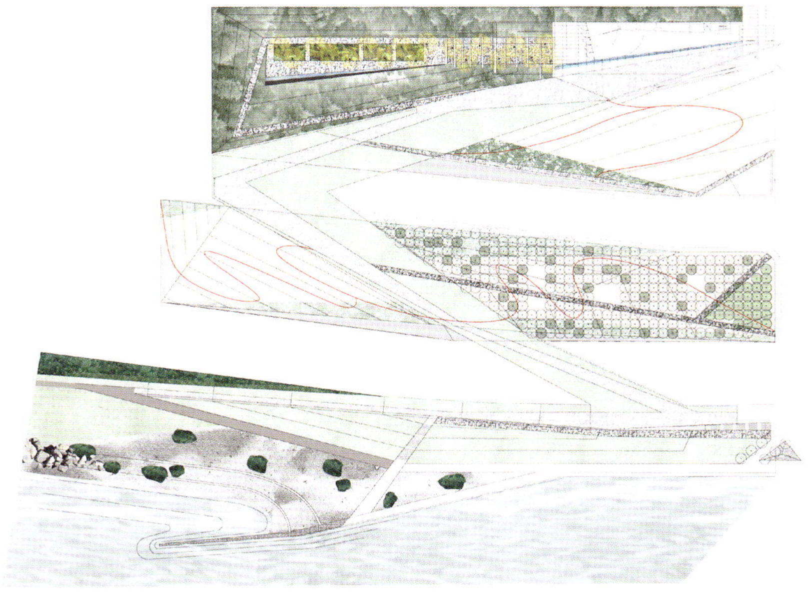

Above clockwise: Initial conceptual sketch of the garden precincts; Plan of schematic design; Section with conceptual images for gardens; An aerial view of the park with city context

I conceived of the gardens as part of the modernist tradition in design, much like Noguchi's California Scenario - but using live ecologies. Each defined garden is a grotesque of the same plant community in the nature lands that surround Seattle. The evergreen forest of the Valley precinct is pulled apart by the valley floor of fossil trees. On one side is the forest, on the other is the forest edge. The Grove, likewise, is like a natural occurring Aspen grove, but in a grid. Its understory will adapt to this grid as it would be any grove in our nature lands. The gardens will adapt to the degree that the caretakers allow, preferably for a Smithson-like entropic nature, rather than cultured horticulture.

—Charles Anderson

Facing: Lupines and satin flower blooming in the meadow
Left: Pre-cast concrete walls with the aspens of the Grove behind

Facing above and below: View of the Valley with Richard Serra's Wake and drifts of yellow ginkgo leaves
Above: Aspen trees of the Grove

Image: Understory of deer and sword ferns in the Grove

Facing clockwise: Alexander Calder's Eagle with Mt. Rainier in the distance; Calder's Eagle sculpture in winter; Irises of the Grove
Above: Flowering dogwood and red chairs
Right: View of the "Valley"

Facing above: Amphitheater of the "Valley"
Facing below: Red chairs and their shadows
Clockwise from above: View of the Meadow in bloom; Columbine; Dogwood; Amelanchier

Above: View of the shoreline precinct with driftwood
Facing above: Waterfront promenade with rain garden
Facing below: Night view of waterfront promenade

Whatcom Museum of History and Art

BELLINGHAM, WASHINGTON, USA, 2008

In collaboration with Jim Olson, Olson Kundig Architects
First Place: BACM International Design Competition

Millions of years ago, the Pacific Northwest was a vastly different landscape, filled with plants that now seem exotic. The Garden of the Ancients at the Whatcom Art and Children's Museum features plants that are or used to be native to the region. This led to a design concept where a glass light-catcher wall surrounds the inside edge of a new Garden of the Ancients Courtyard.

A single ginkgo tree surrounded by a variety of ferns in the courtyard complements the existing Dawn Redwood in front of the nearby courthouse and creates a lush landscape within the museum courtyard. The long, thin planter at the base of the light-catcher wall features horsetail, one of the oldest of all plants. Petrified wood pieces and very large boulders of olivine stone complete the story of an ancient garden.

Protected by the museum building, and accessible from Grand Avenue, this garden's flexible open space will generously accommodate performances and events, while providing an intimate and relaxing atmosphere for Museum visitors.

The "Garden of the Ancients" was conceived as part of the building. It was carved out of the building in the earliest conceptual phase of the design compeititon. The goal was to create a place that served multiple uses, but always in the company of living fossils - ancient plants, massive boulders, petrified wood - and light caught by the wall.

—Charles Anderson

Image: Rendering of proposed museum

Three images above clockwise: Aerial view showing new building's relationship to the other iconic buildings of Bellingham; Interior view of light-catcher wall with portals to garden; Light-catcher wall reflecting evening sky
Facing above: Multipurpose terrace and light-catcher wall
Facing below: Illustrative Site Plan

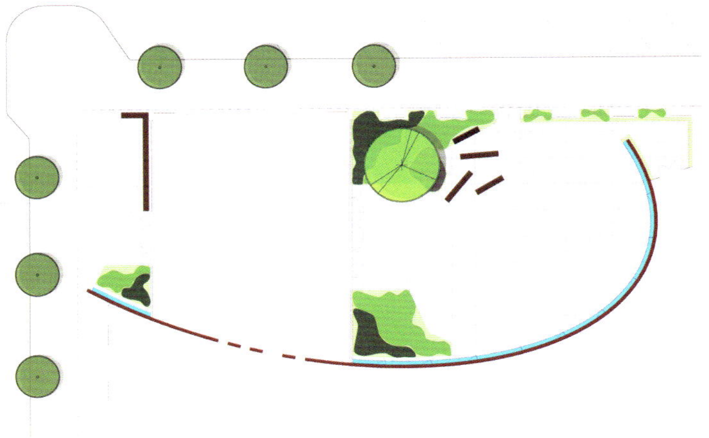

Facing clockwise: Solitary ginkgo tree is the matriarch of the Garden of the Ancients; Ginkgo leaves; Shade-loving horsetail
Above: Proposed image of video performance
Right: Proposed roof garden

Denver Art House

DENVER, COLORADO, USA, 2008

In collaboration with Jim Olson, Olson Kundig Architects

The design of this three-acre residence is inspired by the Denver landscape of mountains and great plains. Emphasizing changing seasonal color, expansive use of native plants, and the fusion of landscape art and architecture, the design creates outdoor rooms, frames views to the surrounding landscape, and makes spaces for sculpture. Meandering paths offer a place to wander through aspen forest, open wildflower prairie, and sculptures. A series of small and large terraces provide places to spend time outside, entertain and watch the seasons change.

The excavation needed to create a firm foundation and basement in a high water table area was substantial. This excess material was used to create a great mound that meanders through specimens of very big conifer trees. The mound was planted in aspens, a landscape in contrast to the lawns and meadows elsewhere on the project. The aspen grove embraces the rear and side yard of the site, while around front open grasses and meadows make every view from inside of the home a different experience. Native and native-compatible species are the dominant plants for this project; however, as the landscape nears the home, a more exotic manicured landscape prevails as complement to the extensive "civilized wilds".

Above: The rabbit sculpture from inside the house tempts the residence fox. Red twig dogwood fills the foreground and shows its red colored twigs in winter
Below: The drive to the house first orients you to the main entry, then curves away to make the drive appear longer
Facing: The great stonewall divides the public and private sides of the house. The gardens are more structured and ornamental on the public side

Above: The curving entry drive directs visitor's views sequentially through landscape around the house
Facing above: View across meadow. Ponderosa pines and two mature American elms are part of the meadow landscape
Facing below: The water feature is a black cube of granite that reflects everything around it and offers the soothing sound of precious water in this arrid landscape

Denver is a difficult place for trees to grow. Its prairie character and the extremes of the weather make it suitable for only the hardiest of plants. We protected a number of existing large trees and we imported a whole new forest of aspen trees. We kept the remnants of a gigantic waterfall feature in the new forest, partly to reveal the site's history, but mainly because a fox lived in its rocks. The client loved rabbits and had quite a collection of hare art and sculpture. The fox lives outside - the eternal antagonist to its prey.

—Charles Anderson

Above: The meadow steps to the lawn are almost consumed by the meadow grasses. The remnant boulders are interplanted with native herbaceous plants
Left: The water feature from the previous garden is now a refuge for a resident fox. This rocky feature is also home for two large bristle cone pines, one of the oldest living trees on earth
Facing above: View of gardens from enclosed porch
Facing below: Master landscape site plan

1. Lawn
2. Great Meadow
3. Black Granite Water Feature with Sculpture
4. Fox Habitat
5. The Stroll
6. Meadow Steps
7. Aspen Stairs
8. Conversation Point
9. Daffodils
10. Oak Grove
11. Auto Court
12. Secret Garden
13. Red Twiggery
14. Big Oak
15. Welcome
16. Pines
17. Aspens
18. Great Terrace

Facing above: Entertainment lawn and patio with meadow beyond. This rectangular lawn is sized to accommodate entertainment tents
Facing below: View from "conversation point" in the aspen forest. This is a very sunny and highest place in the garden
Above: The serpentine wall defines the boundary between manicured lawn and meadow. The "Stroll" is the pathway that meanders through the meadow and circumnavigates the property
Right: Detail of serpentine wall where lawn and meadow meet. Over three thousand bulbs of daffodils were planted in broad swaths to bloom in every spring before the grasses grow tall

Facing above: Stairway leads to aspen forest. This lighting was used to help eliminate the mirror-effect when looking out from inside of the house
Facing below: "Aspen stair" leading out of the aspen grove. The stairway climbs the hill alongside a large existing cedar
Above clockwise: Stairway leading into aspen grove; Native columbine f lower; Potentilla; Hawthorne in bloom

Hanoi Hotel and Convention Center

HANOI, VIETNAM, 2007-2011

In collaboration with Carlos Zapata Studio

Building upon the hotel's dragon concept, the landscape is an abstraction of a Vietnamese creation myth. The landscape concept incorporates the divided "children" of land and water in different ways. Groves of trees in the courtyard represent the land children and the lotus plants (in immersed pots) are the water children.

The convention center landscape is a striking contrast to the landscape adjacent to the hotel. The design is straightforward and considers the heavy use of this area, particularly in regard to buses. From the street moving towards the building, visitors will pass through bands of different trees, ending with palm trees lining the front of the building façade. The palms are not intended to screen the building, but to provide a colonnade of shade and tropical foliage.

Above: Master plan
Below: View from Convention Center
Facing above: Image showing the setting of the "dragon" buildling in the forest
Facing below: View of building on lake with lotus planting

Knowing that the architects referenced a rising dragon with their building, we drew upon a Vietnamese creation story featuring a dragon. The abstraction of those metapors provides structure and poetry to a site plan firmly rooted in this incredible place.

—Charles Anderson

Facing above: Conceptual cardboard model depicting palm-filled courtyard
Above: View of building set in context
Right: Hotel entry water feature

John E. Jaqua Academic Center for Student Athletes

UNIVERSITY OF OREGON, EUGENE, OREGON, USA, 2009

Designed for PHIT, the development arm of Nike founder Phil Knight, in collaboration with Zimmer Gunsul Frasca Architects

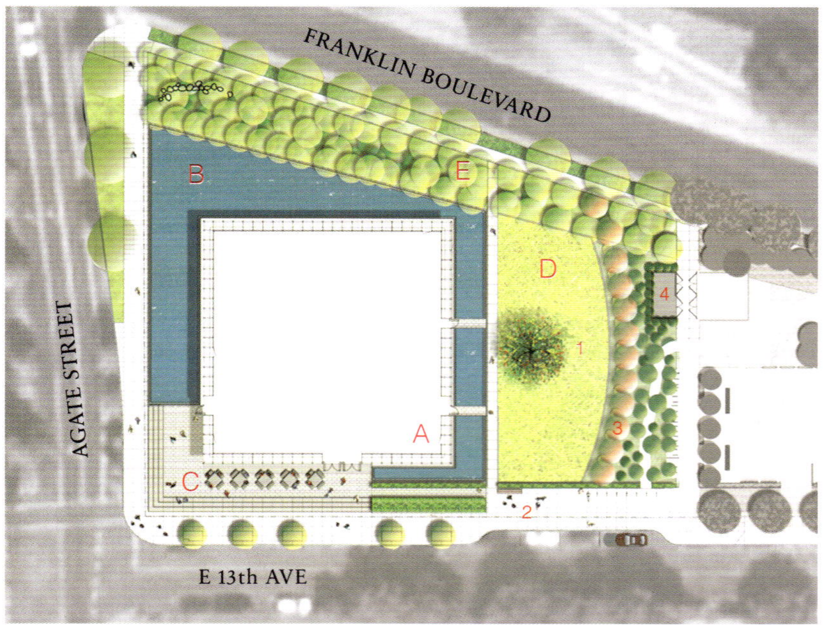

The new John E. Jaqua Academic Center at the University of Oregon is a glass box in a glass box, on a black table of water, with birches. It is a manifestation of pure minimalist architecture and landscape architecture, with a twist. Urban ecology is the functional grounds for the living landscape. In this way, the yin yang relationship between site and building is clear and determined. The static glass façade reflects all the seasonal changes and atmosphere of its context, while the landscape of mostly native plants, arranged in very orderly patterns, contains all the elements and diversity of a robust "natural" landscape.

The setting and the building are complementary. With walls of glass, the interior rooms borrow scenery directly from landscape, while the landscape uses the glass façade as a reflective backdrop. The strong geometric planes of walkways, plazas, and reflecting pool stretch beyond themselves, to integrate interior, exterior, and natural spaces into a seamless whole.

The raised granite terrace and black table of water evocatively capture the classic modernist conceit by breaking down the membrane between indoors and out. Yet the tables of water go beyond that, to mediate between the land, the birches, and the sky, and to harmonize and funnel each into the building's interior. This is the ultimate arrival sequence. The raised plinth of the building distills the visitor's initial landing into one unified gesture, connecting arrival, entry, and an expansive release into landscape.

A black reflective plane of water surrounds the building on four sides and is edged by an elegant linear grove of white birch trees and native shrubs. The birches and associated plant community are the biofiltration system for the project. A gracious, stone entry plaza flanking the south side of the building provides a sunny place for students to congregate and also establishes the strong plinth of the building. Located at a major entrance to the University of Oregon campus, the Glass Box in Glass Box on Black Table of Water with Birches will be a signature building and a departure from the traditional campus landscape.

Above: The reflecting pool tempers the air flowing between the two glass skins of the building
Left: Master landscape site plan
Facing: The pathways to the secondary card-keyed entrances are black granite stone that appear to float on the pool

A. Academic Center
B. Table of Water
C. Terrace
D. Sanctuary
E. Birch Forest
1. Specimen Katsura
2. Bench
3. Dogwood
4. Mechanical

When PHIT (the development arm of Nike founder Phil Knight) contacted me to join the design team, I couldn't imagine what we would be designing. It turned out to be the perfect project to build on the experiences I had gained from the recently completed Olympic Sculpture Park and Tables of Water Residence. We developed a minimalist parti with an ecologically based garden of mostly native plants.

—Charles Anderson

Below: This twilight view of the project reveals its minimalist intent. The mirror of the black table of water equally reflects the rhythms of the building facade and the birch forest
Facing above: Sitting beside the terrace, the entry sign is a complimentary contrast to the minimalism prevailing on site. As the building rests on water, so does the sign on the hedge
Facing below: Each birch on the edge of the black table of water is lit individually, reducing the mirror-effect to the windows on the interior

JOHN E JAQUA
ACADEMIC CENTER
FOR STUDENT ATHLETES

Above: This Katsura tree is the matriarch of the site, centered on the view from the primary conference room. Its stature will one day rival the building

Above: This hedge portal is announced by an enormous bench of Alaska Yellow Cedar. The yellow of this Northwest native tree sits in front of the green of the hedge, representing the school's team colors

Facing above: The building is two feet above the street, revealed here at the table of water's infinity edge. The sharp angle of the corner forces our perspective and challenges our perception of the site
Facing left below: The slim pool on the front side of the building is a suggestion of the abundance of water that surrounds the other three facades. The hedge softens the view out from the building
Facing right below: The plane of the table of water continues on as the lawn in the Sanctuary
Above: The infinity edge along the building cools the air chamber between the building's two glass facades
Below: The inside corner of the infinity edge coping is a single, fabricated piece of granite

Above: The hedge defines the public street edge of the project, setting it off from the lawn in The Sanctuary. The turf is both an icon of athletic play and a respite for hard-working student-athletes
Below: University of Oregon's iconic O becomes a bike rack when in use and a sculpture when not. The solid-steel O's are sand cast and shot-blast finished

Above: The bioswale in the Birch Forest is planted with grasses, shrubs, and trees that adapt well to inundation. The city commented that this is the best looking, and functioning, bioswale that they have ever seen

Zhongkai Sheshan Villas (Shanghai Villas)

SHANGHAI, CHINA, 2005-2011

In collaboration with Olson Kundig Architects

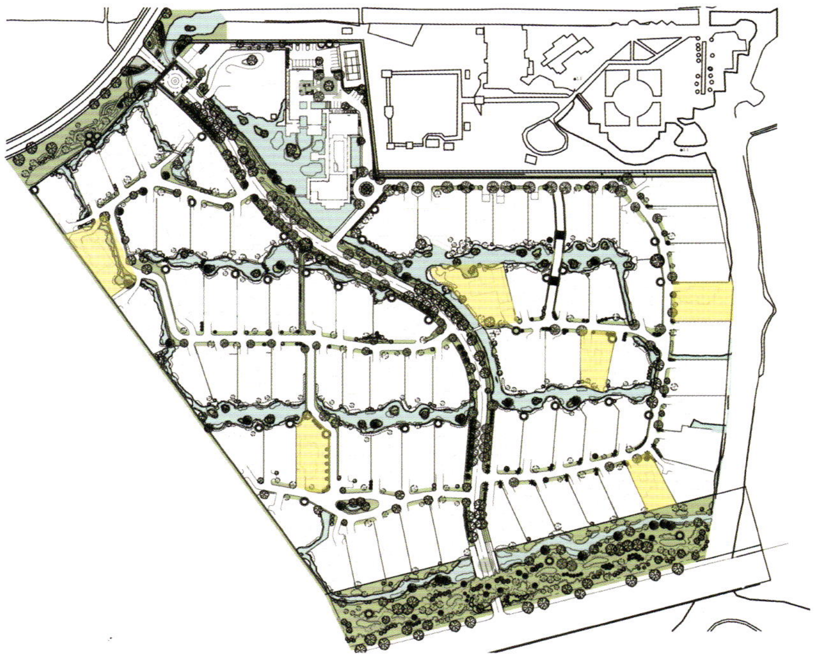

The Zhongkai Sheshan Villas are located in the mountainous terrain of Shanghai's only forest. The forest is an extension of the Tianmushan Mountain Range in the Zhejiang Province, which is noted for its beautiful scenery and has become a hub for high-end home development. The residences are organized into neighborhood clusters, and the plan adopts New Urbanist principles, state-of-the-art technology, and Chinese spatial traditions.

Working with each of the partners of Olson Kundig Architects, CALA designed the landscapes for six of the 79 villas. Incorporating both Chinese and Western influences, the landscapes created unique and contemporary gardens and site features that respond to the architecture and surrounding region. Water features with soothing sounds, gardens highlighting exotic plants, and indigenous stone details helped create a respite from the city for each villa.

Each site within the Villas has a custom-designed home and landscape. We merged Feng Shui and minimalist modernist design principals. Efficiency, balance and beauty were the measure of our efforts. Our visit to the nearby Sheshan Mountains, site of the first Catholic church in Asia, was requisite in beginning our work. This western church sat on top of the mountain, ignoring a core principal of feng shui, but somehow remaining reverent of its site. When our villas are built, I hope that the synergy of the landscape and architecture will likewise be greater than either alone.

—Charles Anderson

Above: Site plan
Below: Backyard of villa E18
Facing: The courtyard at villa W33 is composed of floating planes of water, grass, and paving

POTENTIAL COURTYARD ENTRANCES:

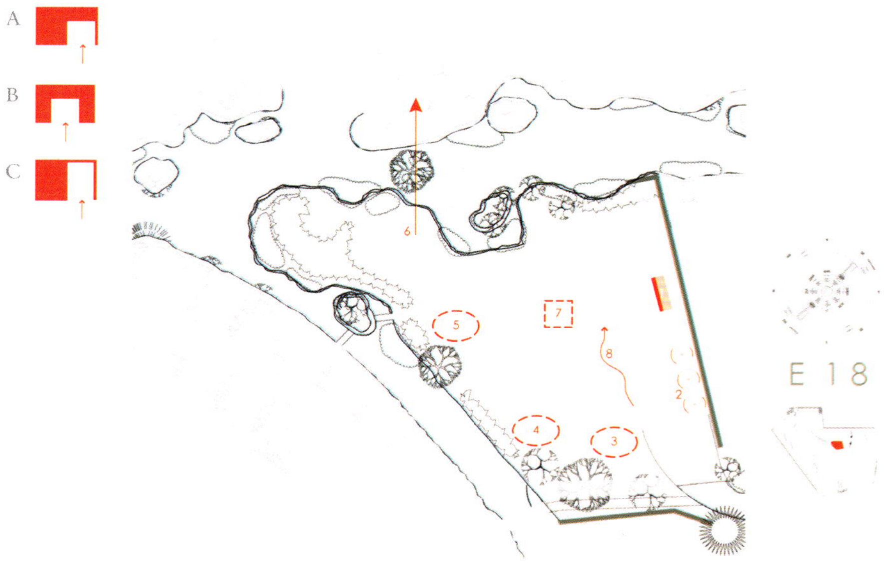

SITE QUALITIES:
o Water to the north
o Possible central house location
o Front entrance facing south
o Trees planted to the north
o Stream to the south
o Road to the west
o Located at the merging of two streams

POTENTIAL SITE QUALITIES TO IMPROVE/CONSIDER:
1 Water feature to the east
2 Fruit trees with vegetable patch to the southeast
3 Element of fire to the south
4 Focus on earth to the southwest
5 Metal, or play-area to the west
6 A mountain-like feature to the north (view of Sheshan Mt. or a tall structure)
7 An open area (courtyard) in the center of the lot
8 Curved path to front entrance

Additional Screen

Facing above and below: Analysis of villa E18 and site plan
Above: Backyard view of villa E25
Right: Dinner terrace at villa E37

Chapel in the Woods

BELLEVUE, WASHINGTON, USA, 2007-2012

In collaboration with Tadao Ando Architect + Associates and Olson Kundig Architects

The landscape of the chapel site frames a clearing in the forest: a place of solace, a counterpoint to the city's cacophony, and a spiritual retreat that exalts in the solitude and beauty of the natural world. The dark, evergreen, processional drive focuses the visitor by contrasting markedly with the surrounding landscape. As this space peels away, visitors step onto an altar surrounded by drifts of white blooms, where the chapel itself rests. Native cherry trees, kousa dogwoods, and other native white-blooming species blow in the wind, enhancing the hilltop prow's sense of airy, ascendant heights, and capitalizing on the magisterial view of Lake Washington and the Cascades to the north. From within the chapel, the still reflections in the water feature, a pastiche of cloud and blossoms, will merge site and sky, heaven and earth. A lone beech tree, an acolyte from the current site, will remain sensitively nested next to the building. Above the chapel, the sanctuary garden will feature reclaimed rhododendrons from the existing site, representing, literally and figuratively, the promise of new life.

Setting a concrete structure in a beautiful forest is contrast enough, but more so since the road leading to the chapel is lined with a stunning allée of Dawn Redwoods, conifers that loose their needles in a rusty drop. The reflecting pool side is also lined with a cloud of white flowering native trees. Every tree plays a part in the seasonal drama of a chapel in the woods.

—Charles Anderson

Above: Site plan
Below left: White-flowering trees accentuate the drama of a foggy day, as seen from inside the chapel
Below right: View through the altar windows on a clear day
Facing: Allée of dawn redwoods at entrance to the chapel

The Anchorage Common

AT THE ANCHORAGE MUSEUM AT RASMUSON CENTER, ANCHORAGE, ALASKA, USA, 2003-2010

In collaboration with David Chipperfield Architects
2008 WASLA Design Award

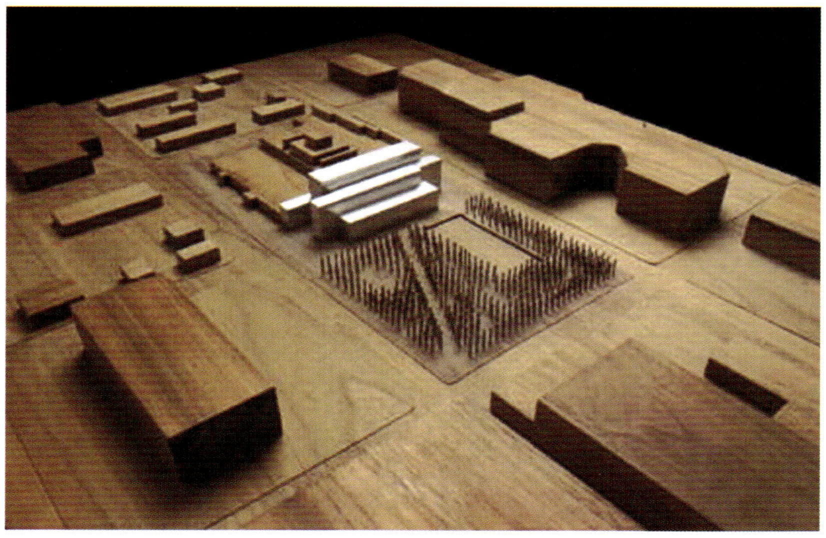

The new landscape for the Anchorage Common lies in the heart the city's downtown. It will serve as a public common and park, exhibition space, and recreational site for the city. Its dual nature requires a design that is at once flexible and dynamic, and creates a strong sense of place and identity. Reflecting the natural history of Alaska's Southcentral region, the concept for the Museum's civic space emerged from the expansive mudflats and deciduous birch forests around Anchorage.

The landscape encompasses the site with a semi-transparent screen of birch trees. This grid of birches starts with tightly-spaced multi-stem trees to the west and loosens up toward the building, with single-stem trees and increased spacing. This urban forest affords the park a sense of openness and visibility, while also creating a striking presence at the street. Its distilled structure provides a continuous framework that will inspire and accommodate art and host a diverse set of celebrations and activities throughout the year. The design for the streetscape considers view corridors, connections to downtown Anchorage and nearby parks, a transit stop, vehicular drop offs, pedestrian access throughout the year, and safety concerns. The landscape creates an identity for the museum that is evident and unique from the street, yet is in keeping with the city's regional context.

Anchorage is surrounded by mountains, mudflats, and great forests. We gathered up these places and made them a part of the new landscape for the museum - we even lit the ice rink to be suggestive of the northern lights. In a land where a clever entrepreneur can sell "firearms and fine antiques," surely one can find room for fine art and wilderness in the heart of the most urban place in Alaska.

—Charles Anderson

Above: Model with street context
Below: Birch trees and building façade
Facing: Evening view of frosted birch trees against the fritted glass façade. Steps lead to the promenade and the museum's main entrance

ANCHORAGE MUSEUM
AT RASMUSON CENTER

Above: This aerial view of the common shows both the increasing density of birch trees from the building across the Common and the angular geometry of the walkway superimposed over the curvilinear walk of the birches
Left: The drama of frosted birches is accentuated by the reflection of the setting sun on the building facade. Wood and concrete benches flank the Green
Facing above: Master landscape site plan
Facing below: Landscape Layers

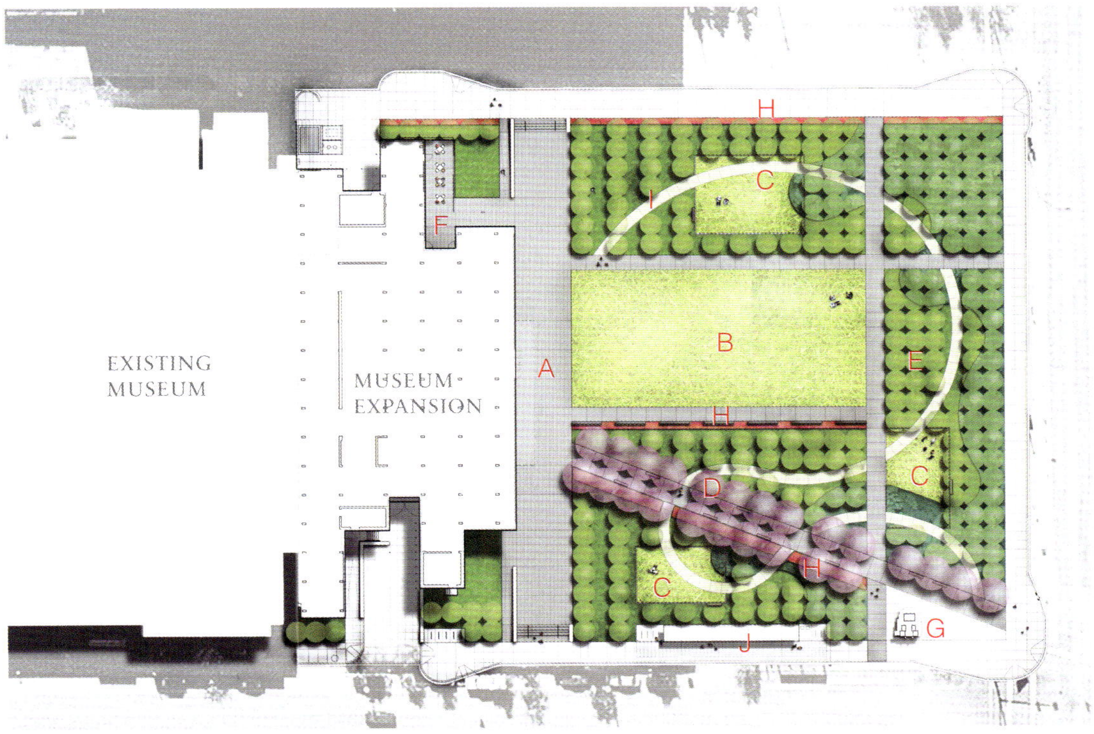

Master landscape site plan
A. Promenade
B. The Green
C. Rooms
D. Allée
E. Birches
F. Cafe
G. Sculpture
H. Annual Flowers
I. Walk of the Birches
J. Transit Stop

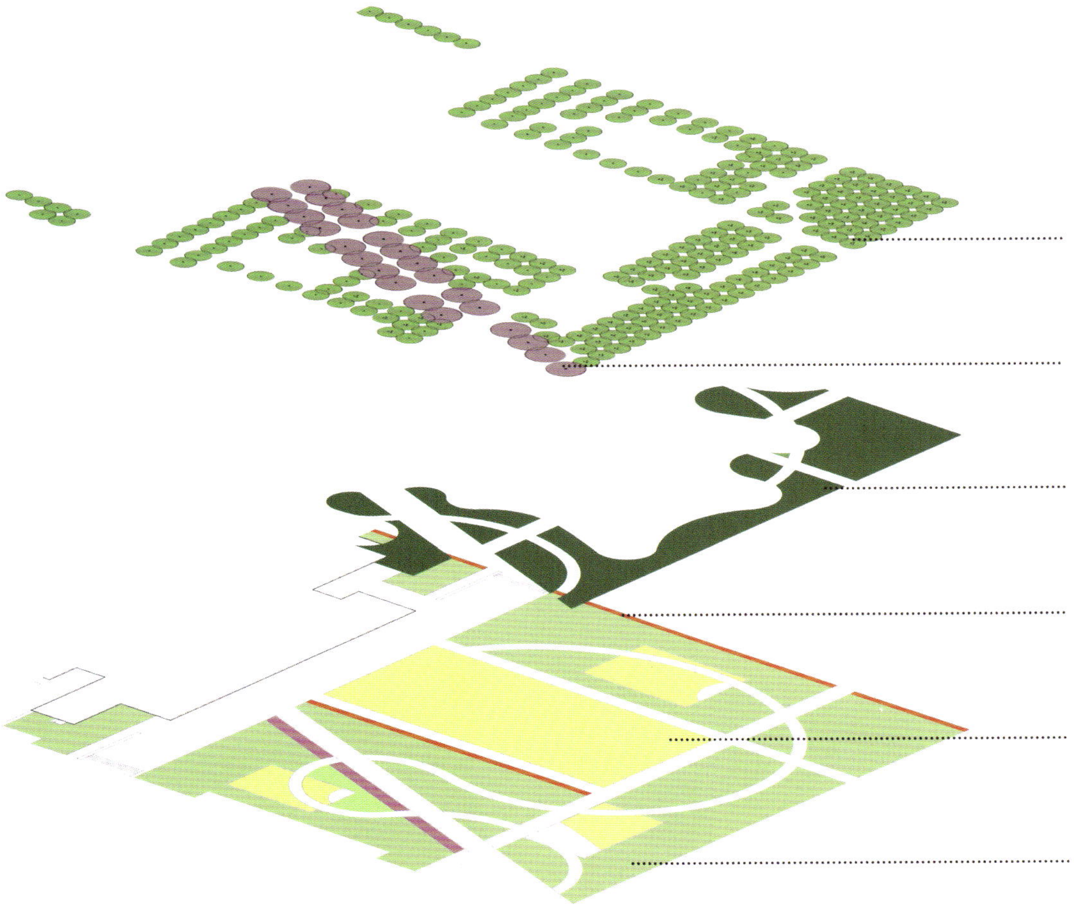

Above: View from downtown Anchorage pedestrian overpass to the museum entrance through the birch forest. Sculpture by Antony Gormley is in the foreground
Left: Concept sketch for the grid of birches
Facing above: View of the great lawn, the heart of the Anchorage Common
Facing below: The Green is a gathering place for community activities and also a tranquil location to observe reflections on the façade

ANCHORAGE MUSEUM

ANCHORAGE MUSEUM

ANCHORAGE MUSEUM
AT RASMUSON CENTER

Facing above: View of entry stairs to promenade. To the left of the steps, the "back of house" functions look aesthetically integrated
Facing below: The dining terrace is an extension of the building's integrally colored concrete foundation. It appears to float above the landscape
Above: Birch trees silhouette against the glass facade between the street and the outdoor café

MUSEUM

Facing above: Birches in early spring. From this vantage point, where the trees are planted most closely, the grid is barely discernible
Facing below: During design development there was concern that the birch trees would be too dense. A mock up of 2 x 2 timbers demonstrated that they were not
Above: The 16-foot ipe benches are a popular place in the sun at lunchtime. A stainless steel ribbon on the back edge of each bench is etched with patron names. The colorful flowers are a major tourist attraction of Anchorage

ANCHORAGE MUSEUM

Facing: Anchorage has a great tradition of extravagant annual flower planting. These flower beds are kept to long linear strips as a counterpoint to the native planting in the other 80 percent of the park
Above: The Walk of the Birches is a black pigmented concrete path seeded with recycled glass. The meandering of this path encourages strolling and discovery
Right: View of "Habitat" by Antony Gormley through birch trees

International Peace Gardens

ON THE MANITOBA/ NORTH DAKOTA BORDER, 2007-2010 (Phase 1)

In collaboration with GPP and Friesen Tokar Architects

Inspired by horticulturalist Henry Moore in 1929, the International Peace Garden Project, on the border between Manitoba and North Dakota, is a symbol of friendship between Canada and the United States. The site consists of 2,400 acres of a temperate forest in what is almost the geographic center of the North American continent. Its location in the Turtle Mountains, rising 900 feet above the plains, is a breathtaking anomaly of aspen, oaks, and lakes overlooking the broad expanse of prairies and wheat fields. Construction of the gardens, structures, and lakes began in the 1930s during the grip of the Great Depression by the US Civilian Conservation Corps. The gardens have grown in subsequent decades with the addition of the 120-foot-tall Peace Towers, the Peace Chapel, and, most recently, steel girders transported from the World Trade Center lying at rest at the 911 Memorial.

Significant improvements are planned over the next five years, including a new visitor center, an international center for peace, a new 250-room lodge, and the revitalization of the historic sunken garden pool and surrounding pleasure gardens. CALA was chosen in 2007 as the landscape architect for these projects. Work included the site planning, site design, and horticultural improvements to the entire gardens.

I cannot imagine a greater anomaly than an immense formal garden in the middle of North America. This one is within 30 miles of my first college experience, where my lifetime career direction as a plantsman was sown. I've come full circle, but it may be more like the lower half of a figure eight. On one site visit, in the dead of winter, the air was so cold that the clear sky snowed, exposed skin would freeze in 10 minutes, and hoar frost stuck to the trees. It's certainly a land of extreme extremes and surprising beauty.

—Charles Anderson

Above: Site plan
Facing: Watercourse leading to sunken garden

Above: Proposed perennial beds
Facing above: Conceptual sketch
Facing below: Aerial view of site under construction

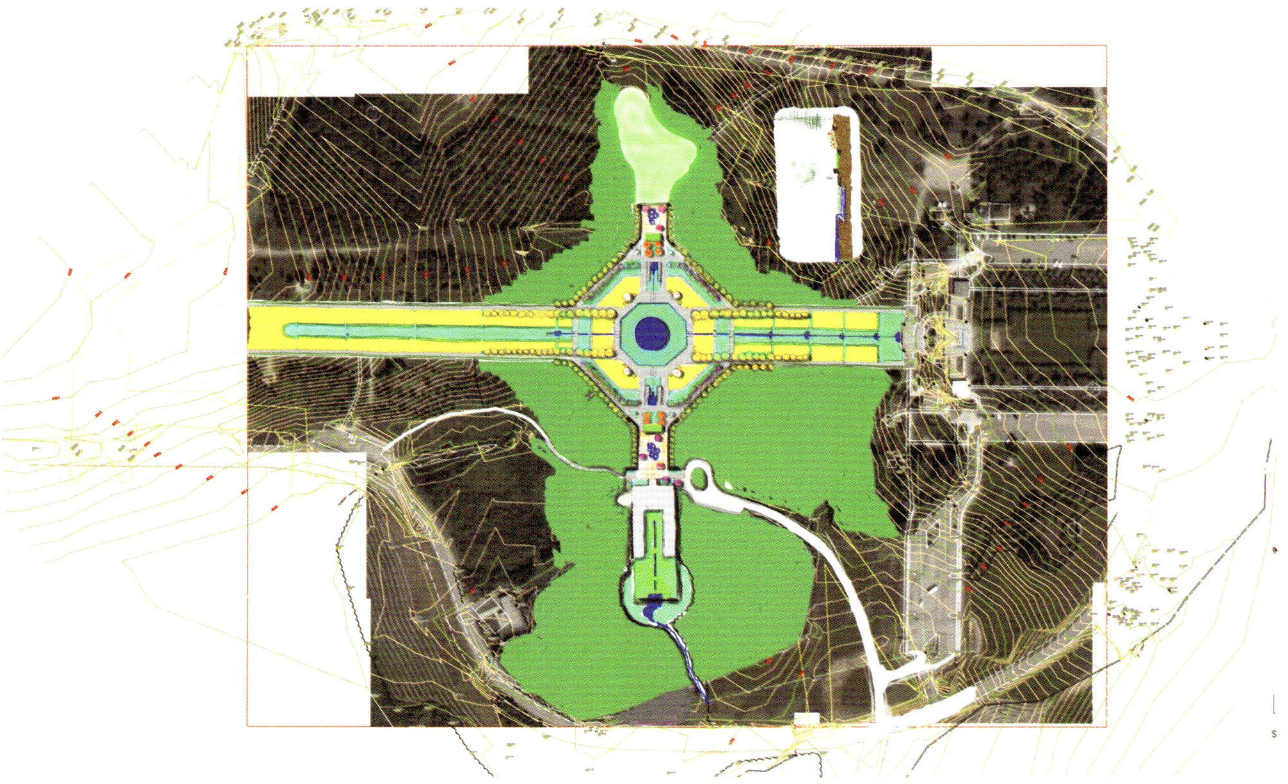

Above: New visitor center and conservatory, with restored WPA- era picnic structure
Left: View across octagon pool to visitor center

Clockwise from top: Octagon pond inscribed by circle of aerator buggles; Subtle bubbles - rather than large jets - aerate the pond to better reflect the spirit of peace; View across the octagon pool, with restored homemakers fountain in foreground

Above: Water course delineating the border of the United States and Canada
Facing: A view from the terrace to water channel and the towers

Lean Linear City / Soleri

INTERNATIONAL, 2009-ONGOING

In collaboration with Paolo Soleri

The Lean Linear City is a project of Paolo Soleri in response to great interest in China and Korea. Using the modules and nodes of linked infrastructure, the landscape explores the relationship of structures to each other and their setting. The reinforcement of horizontal connections between structures and the character of their landscape result in a landscape metaphor that treats the structure like a mountain rising from the plains. The lowest areas are the most sheltered and have the greatest amount of water to utilize. As one moves toward the highest part of the structure, the environmental conditions are contrasted by more wind desiccation, less available water and higher temperature fluctuations.

The vertical gradient determines the kinds of plant communities and gardens sustained within the architecture. To support this idea, the façade is altered by sculpting volumes of three-dimensional spaces to allow for vertical landscapes of trees and other structures within the building. This enhances the integration of the on-the-ground landscapes with the terra level, a mid-level landscape/transportation corridor, which brings large-scale landscape to a midpoint in the architecture and higher. Openings in the façade will make intermittent landscape above and below the terra level.

The circulation system is connected throughout the linear city with a central focus on pedestrian circulation, conveniently tied to local regional and world transport systems. Pedestrian connections knit each side of the module together with a series of bridges, which traverse the grand central landscape at the core of each module. The central landscape supports an extensive water harvesting, nutrimental gardens, and a vast array of civic spaces. It contains mostly native riparian plants that assist with bio-filtration and remediation of stormwater runoff and other urban processes. This flexible, dynamic, ecologically-based landscape furthers our connections to the setting by respecting wildlife corridors with enhanced habitat. The landscape on the outside edges of each module are a combination of preservation lands, agriculture and large-scale recreational facilities.

Seeing the architecture as a setting for readily-accessible urban open space ensures a variety of landscape expressions that enrich and reconnect our lives to the natural ecological evolving processes. Simply put, the hummingbird will be just as at home as we are in this evolving, yet familiar, urban/agrarian city.

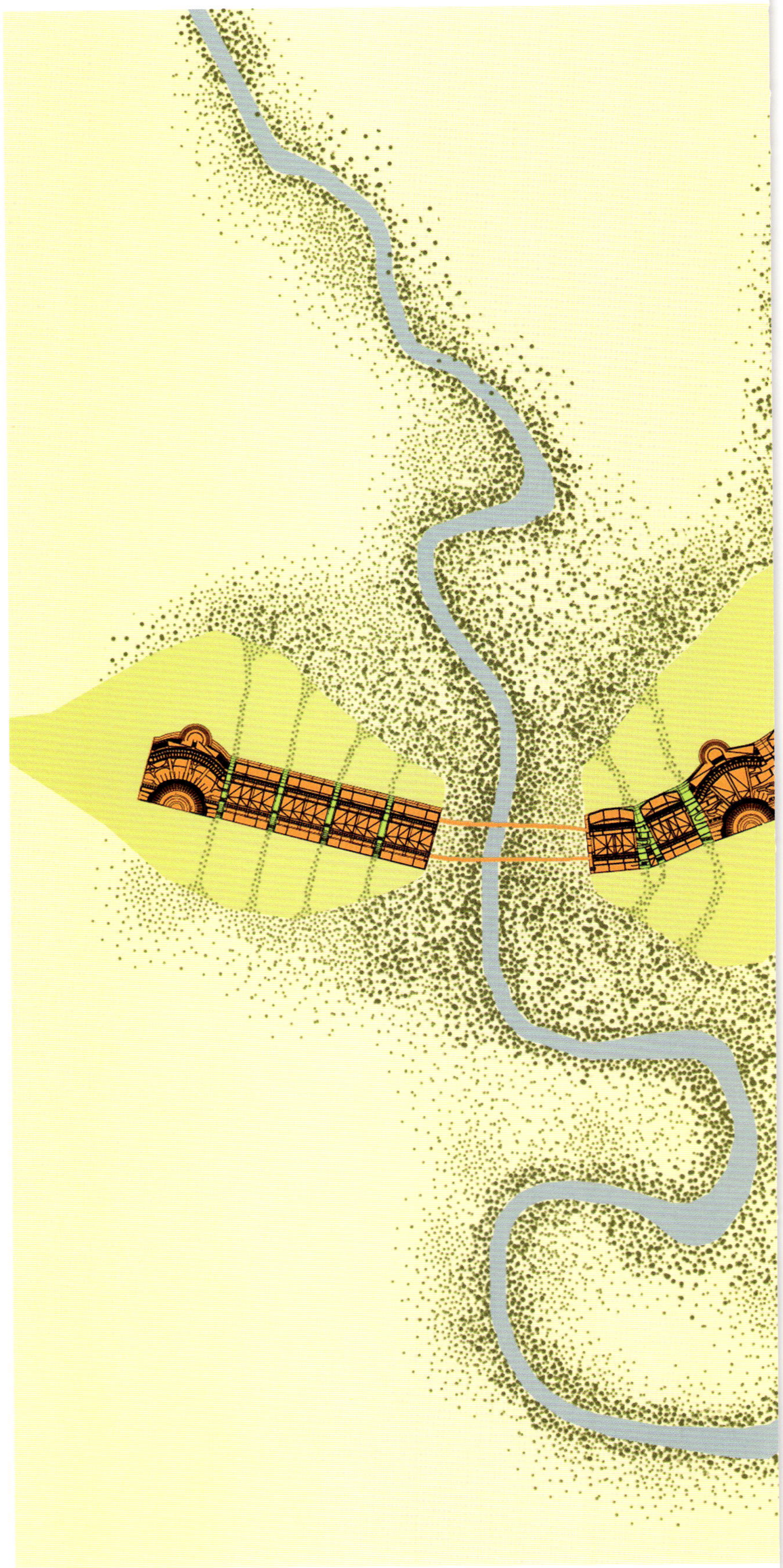

Image: Site diagram

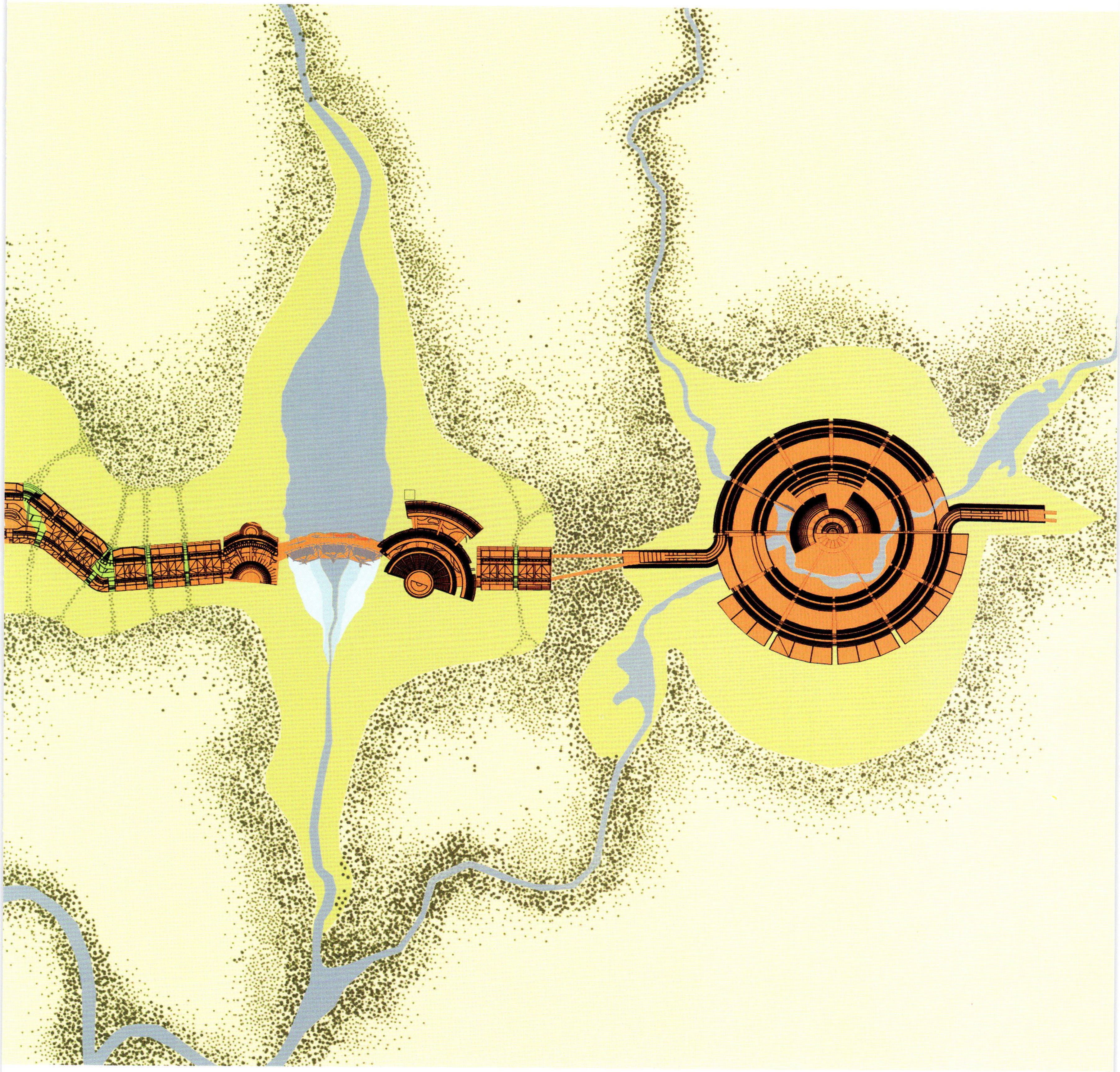

Above: Conceptual landscape master plan for segment of linear city
Facing above: Environmental analysis and microclimate study
Facing below: Land use proposal

Paolo Soleri's books on Arcologies have always been a critical part of my library. His work, Buckminster Fuller's, and LeCorbusier's all espoused an alternative and more vital way of life. My ongoing work with Soleri's associates, especially Tomiaki Tumura, is fulfilling a lifelong dream and is now a part of my journey.

—Charles Anderson

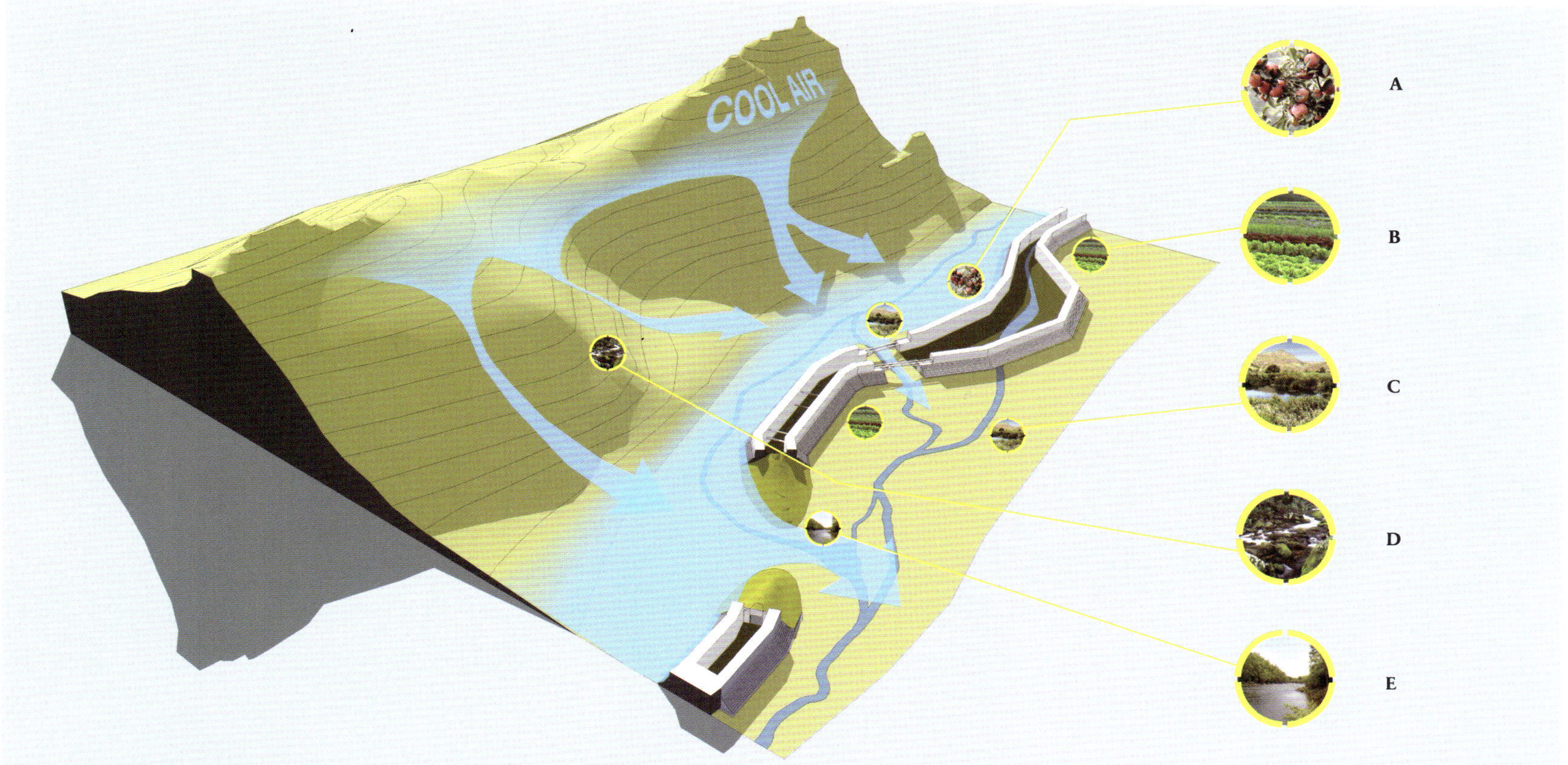

A. Apple and Pear **Orchards** utilize cool air reservoirs to achieve necessary chilling hours in warmer days
B. Specific agriculture plots are situated to best exploit the architectures micro-climates, extending seasons and expanding crop diversity
C. Urban waste-water is polished for groundwater re-charge by a network of constructed and enhanced **wetlands.** In addition to this engineering benefit, a foundation for regional biodiversity is established
D. To stabilize local hydrology and soils **tributaries** are preserved, enhanced or restored to a resilient and productive state. Once secured these corridors can be used for wilderness access
E. River corridors are allowed generous buffers for flood protection and wildlife passage

Above: View of building alcove
Below: Conceptual diagram showing the mountain plant communities best adapted to the microclimates created by the building form
Above: Sequence of potential uses on the terra level

Image: Interior view of Lean Linear City

Hangzhou CBD

HANGZHOU, CHINA, 2009-2012

In collaboration with XWHO International Group

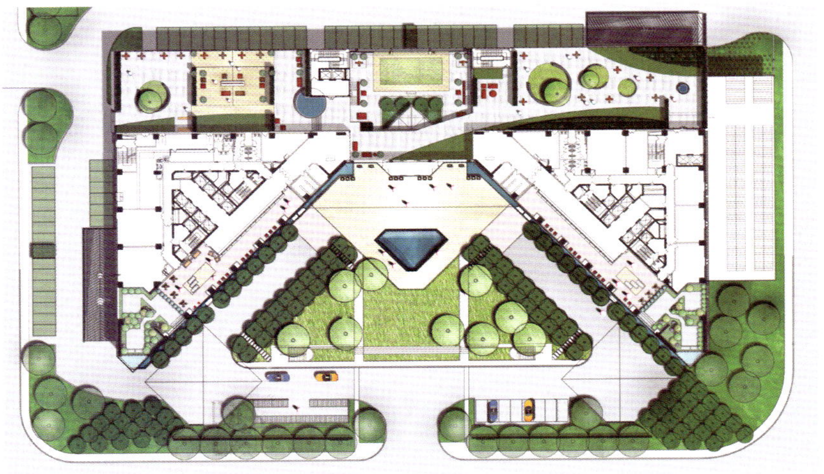

This resort-like setting for residences features two diamond-shaped towers, designed by Gensler Architects. The project is part of a redevelopment effort aimed at creating a new central business district for the city of Hangzhou.

Using a diamond form as a metaphor, the entry garden's central water feature is a black diamond, a reflective water element in a disciplined garden of native trees and grass. The water elsewhere in the project continues a theme of reflective pure tables of water. The Garden of Seasons, the project's central park, provides a place for the guests to stroll and enjoy the outdoors. At the park's core is a great lawn with magnificent Camphor trees that are flanked on two sides with groves of dawn redwoods. The black diamond of water provides the project with a signature element and focal point for the building's entrance.

The building has three distinct roof terraces on its north side. Each of the terraces provides the user with opportunities to enjoy the outdoors. Adjacent to the indoor pool on the third floor is an activity terrace with a multipurpose court. On the fourth floor, there are two gardens. One is designed for large outdoor banquets and events with an outdoor kitchen, a table of fire, and a table of water. The other provides a park-like atmosphere for guests to walk their dogs and children to play on the turf landforms. The fourth-floor terraces capture views of a nearby park and the Qiantang River.

Above: Site plan
Below: Entrance with camphor trees
Facing: Aerial view

This is my seventh project in China. The core approach to my design there has always been to bring a sensitivity that is ecologically based, modern, minimalist, and as Chinese as possible. This means working with my associated host designers and clients to give them an appreciation for landscape as a part of the urban history of China while bringing my personal style and signature to the project. When I first arrived in China, on the first day I sensed a familiarity with the land, like I had been here before and that I knew the people from a previous time.

—Charles Anderson

Facing: Roof garden and dining terrace
Above: Roof garden and family terrace, with raised planters to increase soil depth for trees

Fraternal Twins

BELLEVUE, WASHINGTON, USA, 2007-2010

In collaboration with Olson Kundig Architects

This Lake Washington residence features a series of gardens that create outdoor rooms with strong relationships with the interior. The Entry Garden is meant to be beautiful and easy to maintain. Passing through the entry gate, elegant trees and a simple shrub and groundcover palette create a threshold between the neighborhood and the house. Filled with spectacular plants with big leaves and lots of color evocative of tropical climates, the Tropical Garden is the showcase garden that surrounds the main entrance, elevated glass family room, and water feature. In contrast to the Tropical Garden, The Sanctuary is an intimate garden that features plants known for their bloom, structure, or fragrance. A small, round water feature, with one discrete water jet, fills the garden with the sound of dancing water. Native plant restoration along the shoreline is the feature of the garden along the shore.

The name Fraternal Twins comes from the two houses in the garden. The client owned and lived on one lot and purchased a neighboring lot to expand their home for entertaining. The new house is the fraternal twin of the existing one. The DNA they share is their mirror footprints, the paint, and the landscape.

We forested the street side and added the tropics garden, the rhododendron garden, and the sanctuary. The L-shape of both homes form the enclosure for the great lawn. The clients were gracious and appreciative of the landscape. We reused a great number of specimen trees and large shrubs from the two very different lots and merged them with a minimalist vision - putting a twist on a very modernist design.

—Charles Anderson

Above: Site plan
Below: Linear stairway and lawn tie together the two separate houses
Facing: Reflecting pool and tropical garden

Image: Generously-sized lawn for entertaining

Inn at the Market Courtyard

SEATTLE, WASHINGTON, USA, 2009

The renovations to the Inn at the Market Courtyard in Seattle's Pike Place Market aimed to create a contemporary and inviting space for hotel guests and the public. By replacing the old brick paving with light colored pavers, updating the water feature with dark granite, and selecting new site furnishings, the courtyard transformed into a plaza. The new space draws people in from the streets and presents visitors with great shops, a cozy setting and views to Puget Sound.

Above and below: View of interior courtyard
Facing: Café seating in courtyard

CAMPAGNE

This courtyard was formerly made of red brick like the building. It had a dark quality that made the place feel wet and cold. We brought light into the courtyard by simply changing the pavement to light tan color with a contrasting black water feature. We added elegant benches and planters to transform this very urban courtyard into a light-filled amenity to one of Seattle's most iconic of places.

—Charles Anderson

Facing: Water feature with sculpture
Above: Courtyard with restaurant dining area
Right: Bench with metal planters

South Coast Plaza

COSTA MESA, CALIFORNIA, USA, 2001

In collaboration with Kathryn Gustafson

The South Coast Plaza complex is one of the nation's premier retail centers and Orange County's performing arts quadrangle. The Strata Garden is designed as an interpretation of human and geologic time scales. The 24,000 square foot terrace and café dining area at the eastern end of the 560 feet bridge of Gardens connects two retails centers that comprise South Coast Plaza. The Flying Bridge takes the shape of bird in flight as it lifts off from the garden that supports a carpet of bougainvillea. The plaza displays the geologic dynamics of the area by the use of layers of stone and by air bubbling from the floor to animate the water feature.

Above: Site plan
Below: Proposed image of terrace
Facing: View of "Bridge of Gardens"

Kathryn Gustafson brought this project to our office, as a collaboration between her, my office, and the architect. It was one of the most highly anticipated shopping mall projects I had ever heard of in a very well-to-do part of California. What amazes me most about the work is the craft and exquisite detailing of the "strata" stone walls and stairs, something that I will always admire.

—Charles Anderson

Facing: Detail of bougainvillea growing on bridge
Above: View of inside and outside of "Bridge of Gardens"
Below: Shade structure on bridge

Facing above: Stairway revealing the strata of stone layers
Facing below: Edge detail of water features
Above: Air entrained water of upper water feature
Right: Air-entrained water represents seismic activity

3031 Western Avenue

SEATTLE, WASHINGTON, USA

In collaboration with Mott Hinthorne Architects

3031 Western Avenue is a luxury high-rise apartment project situated on the northern edge of Seattle's Olympic Sculpture Park and looking out to Puget Sound. It lies in a transition zone between a dense urban community, commercial use and a public waterfront promenade. By virtue of its location and the adjacent uses the current views are preserved in perpetuity. Architectural skin detailing and glass "veils" play to the views and green screens of trelliswork extend the gardens of the sculpture park to soften and blur the edge between garden and building.

The landscape program required improved pedestrian access and capitalization on natural and urban views. There are two landscapes on this site - one is at street level and the other is a roof garden fourteen stories in the air. At street level the section of Bay Street between Elliot and Western Avenues was vacated and presented an opportunity for an urban promenade. Plaza space lies over an underground garage ramp entrance and a grand set of steps creates a forced perspective toward the water.

Three trays of garden plantings descending along the steps hold and release rain water after storms. The plaza has space for sculpture. Flowering trees and autumn color provide moments of seasonal change.

The roof garden extends the modernist grid to create proportioned spaces for summer social events. It takes advantage of stunning views overlooking the Olympic Sculpture Park and Puget Sound. A lone shore pine landmarks the roof garden - a reference to the shore pine on the rooftop garden on another high-rise a few blocks away.

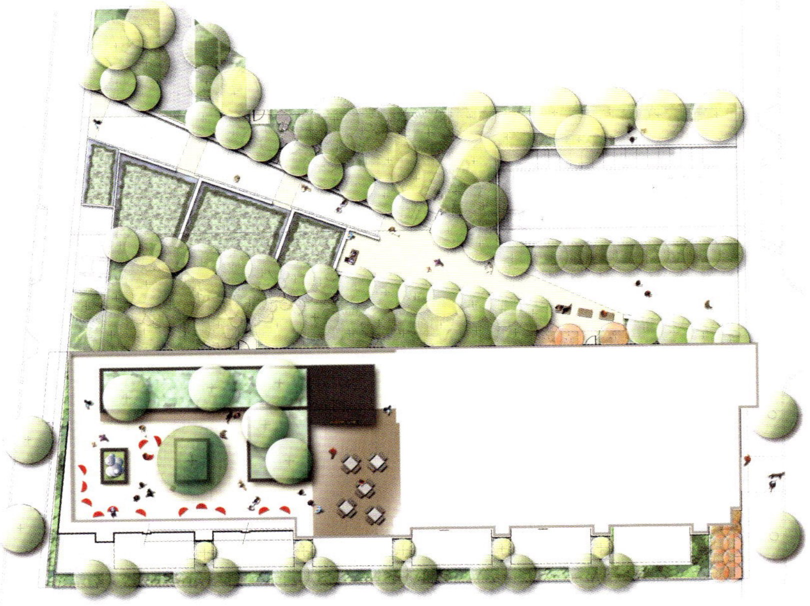

Above: Site plan
Below: Site plan in context

Above: View of grand staircase

Seattle's Olympic Sculpture park has become one of several urban gems. When Erik Mott contacted us to join them on the only piece of underdeveloped land next to the park, I was excited that something significant would be built in that "missing tooth" context. From the earliest discussions while designing the Olympic Sculpture Park we sought to embrace all of the differential edges and adjacencies that would insure diverse visual and audible experiences to the pedestrians. Now we had the chance to secure an unfinished edge with a new building and landscape that will have to do the same "embrace its context"...

—Charles Anderson

Above: View from Olympic Sculpture Park
Facing: View from street

CHARLES ANDERSON, FASLA RESUME

PROFESSIONAL EDUCATION

Masters of Landscape Architecture, Graduate School of Design,
Harvard University, 1985
Bachelors of Landscape Architecture, BSLA,
Washington State University, 1981
Associates in Applied Science, MSU, Dakota College at Bottineau, North Dakota, 1977

PROFESSIONAL EXPERIENCE

Charles Anderson Landscape Architecture; Principal,
Founder; Seattle, WA,
Scottsdale, AZ; 2001 - present
Anderson and Ray; Principal and Co-Founder;
Seattle, WA; 1994 - 2001

PROFESSIONAL REGISTRATION

Washington License #560 - since 1992;
California License #4103 - since 1995;
Arizona License - since 2009;
Alaska License #11366 - since 2005;
Montana License #242 - since 2006;
Oregon License #659 - since 2008

PROFESSIONAL AFFILIATIONS

American Society of Landscape Architects, Fellow, 2007 - present
American Society of Landscape Architects, Member, 1992 - 2007
American Society of Landscape Architects, Affiliate, 1980 - 1992

LECTURES

Urban Ecology, Arizona State University, Herberger Institute for Design and the Arts, Tempe Arizona, 2010
47th International Making Cities Livable Conference, Portland, Oregon, Lecturer, 2009
Xeriscape Council of New Mexico Conference, Lecturer, 2008
Seattle Art Museum – Olympic Sculpture Park, Lecturer, 2007
Global Green Lecture Series, University of Washington, Lecturer and Panel Discussion Member, 2007
2007 ASLA Annual Meeting and Expo, San Francisco, Lecturer, 2007
British Columbia Society of Landscape Architects, Lecturer, 2007
Process Lecture Series, Alaska Design Forum, Fairbanks and Anchorage, Lecturer 2007
Public Workshop, Anchorage Museum of History and Art, Lecturer, 2006
ASLA Annual Meeting and Expo, Minneapolis, Lecturer, 2006
Korean Institute of Landscape Architecture, Seoul National University, Lecturer, 2004
Friends of Olmsted Parks, Seattle, Lecturer, 2003_Seattle Art Museum, Lecturer, 2003
Bellevue Botanical Garden, Lecturer, 2002
Seattle Department of Parks and Recreation City-Wide Education Program, Lecturer, 1999, 2001
University of Washington Center for Urban Horticulture, Lecturer, 1998

TEACHING & JURIES

Arizona State University; Tempe, AZ, Faculty Associate, 2009-2010
ASLA National Student Awards, Juror, 2009
AIA Northwest Chapter, Juror, 2008
University of Washington, Visiting Instructor, 2007
University of Washington, Juror, 2003 - 2007
National Garden Club, Visiting Instructor, 2002 - 2004

PUBLIC SERVICE

Seattle Design Commission, Commissioner, 2003 - 2005
Monorail Review Panel, Design Commission Representative, 2004 - 2005
Seattle Design Commission, Waterfront Planning Subcommittee, 2004 - 2005
Light Rail Review Panel, Environmental Impact Statement Reviewer, 2003
Seattle Arts Council, Advisor, 2003
Seattle Department of Neighborhoods, Ecological Restoration Volunteer, 1994 - 2000

SELECTED PUBLICATIONS AUTHORED

"Viaduct Replacement Gives City a Chance to Make Waterfront Unforgettable." The Seattle Times, December 12, 2008.
"Seattle Designer has a Renaissance in North Dakota." Daily Journal of Commerce, April 17, 2008.
"Landscape Grounded in Northwest Natural History." Daily Journal of Commerce, January 18, 2007.
"Trillium Projects." International New Landscape, April 2006, pp. 78-82.
"Art Meets Frisbees in North Seattle Park." Daily Journal of Commerce, April 22, 2004.
"Celestial Landscapes." Architecture+, July 2004, pp. 96-97.
"Olympic Sculpture Park: A Northwest Collage." Daily Journal of Commerce, April 10, 2003.
"An Evergreen Manifesto." Daily Journal of Commerce, April 18, 2002.
"Inviting Nature Back into the Neighborhood." Daily Journal of Commerce, April 19, 2001.
"Urban Ecology, or Expressing Nature in the City." Daily Journal of Commerce, April 20, 2000.
"Urban Wetlands: Another Approach." Daily Journal of Commerce, August 19, 1999.
"Time Travel on the Terrace." Daily Journal of Commerce, April 1, 1999.
"Outdoor Classrooms: Building a Lake Washington Environmental Education Complex." Daily Journal of Commerce, March 27, 1997.
Anderson, Charles. Native Plant Alliance-Manual of Native Plant Communities, Cascade Biomes, 1995, 1997, 1999.

SELECTED PUBLICATIONS

Featured in the book, 1000X Landscape Architecture, Braun, 2009.
Drew, Hank. "Seattle Design 100+: New 10." Seattle Homes and Lifestyles, January 2009, pp. 52-60.
Gamache, Shawna. "Revamped Paine Field hangar worthy of WWII planes." Daily Journal of Commerce, June 5, 2008.
Enlow, Clair. "Cliff Dwelling: Landscape Architects Re-create a Native Pacific Northwest Landscape in the City." Landscape Architecture, February 2008, pp. 74-81.
Slovan, Margie. "Viaduct Vision Calls for an Open Tunnel with Lids." Daily Journal of Commerce, December 23, 2008.
"WASLA Awards Highlight Local Landscape Restoration." Daily Journal of Commerce, June 18, 2008.
Stahl, Dean. "The Beauty of Basic | Spare Equals Serenity." The Seattle Times, May 18, 2008.
Roth, Bill. "It's a New Museum Piece." Anchorage Daily News, April 25, 2008.
Easton, Valerie. "Scaling Up: For Gardens with Real Vision, See the Trees." The Seattle Times, April 6, 2008.
"Practice in China: CALA." Urban Space Design Magazine, January 2008, pp. 42-44.

"NW Projects Take Top AIA Awards." Daily Journal of Commerce, January 10, 2008.
Brophy, Nicole. "15 to Watch." Estates West, Fall 2008, pp. 62-76.
Easton, Valerie. "Sculpture Park Groundcover." The Seattle Times, February 7, 2007.
Rowe, Lindsay. "Design Achievement Awards '07." Seattle Homes and Lifestyles, October 2007, pp 74-78.
Enlow, Clair. "Art in the Open." Landscape Architecture, August 2007.
"An Urban Incarnation of the Native Landscape: Olympic Sculpture Park." Landscape Design, July 2007, pp. 32-38.
Enlow, Clair. "A Look at Seattle's Great Places, Current and Future." Daily Journal of Commerce, July 25, 2007.
Holt, Gordy. "Landscape Designers and Projects in Seattle Win Awards." Seattle Post Intelligencer, July 18, 2007.
"CALA Wins Award for Sculpture Park." Daily Journal of Commerce, May 2, 2007.
"Reclaiming the Time and Place: Trillium Projects." C3, April 2007, pp. 48-61.
Wingate, Marty. "Landscape Design is Built on Our NW Environment." Seattle Post Intelligencer, January 18, 2007.
Enlow, Clair. "Design Perspectives: A look at Seattle's great places, current and future." Daily Journal of Commerce, January 17, 2007.
Robertson, Iain. "Cultivating the Waterfront." Seattle Post Intelligencer, December 24, 2006.
"Strategies for a Greener Future." Landscape Architecture, November 2006.
Andrews, Jenny. "ASLA Award of Honor: Still Waters." Garden Design, November 2006, p.90.
Bennett, Sam. "Spectacular Site a Challenge for Sculpture Park Designers." Daily Journal of Commerce, November 22, 2006.
"Anderson, Berger New WASLA Fellows." Daily Journal of Commerce, October 18, 2006.
Simons, John Ormsbee and Barry W. Starke. Landscape Architecture a Manual of Environmental Planning and Design. McGraw-Hill, 2006, p. 104.
"Tables of Water." International New Landscape, October 2006, pp. 66-72.
Easton, Valerie. "Inspired by Nature." The Seattle Times, October 8, 2006.
"Mount Saint Helens." International New Landscape, February 2006, pp. 76-81.
Slovan, Margie. "Being an Architect in China Requires Patience, Flexibility." Daily Journal of Commerce, May 3, 2006.
Arab, Michelle. "Creating an Urban Forest in Anchorage." Daily Journal of Commerce, April 27, 2006.
"Designing Seattle's Green Network for the Next Century." Arcade, Fall 2006.
Martin, Frank. "Design for Danger, Confronting the Sublime at Mount St. Helens." Landscape Architecture, June 2006, pp. 136-143.
"Creating Sculpture Park's Landscape is an Art in Itself." Daily Journal of Commerce, September 12, 2005.
"Six Win Top Honors for Landscape Work." Daily Journal of Commerce, November 16, 2005.
"Professional Best: ASLA's 2004 Awards." Landscape Architecture, September 2004, pp. 96-109.
"'SAM Moves Outdoors' with $85m Park." Daily Journal of Commerce, June 7, 2005.
Enlow, Clair. "Cities Can Enjoy Their Past and Future." Daily Journal of Commerce, February 2, 2005.
"Tides and Trees to Mark Anchorage Museum Landscape." Daily Journal of Commerce, November 3, 2004.
"Trillium Projects Win for Native Plant Use." Daily Journal of Commerce, August 18, 2004.
Enlow, Clair. "Narrating History with Natives." Landscape Architecture, July 2004, pp. 46-59.
Enlow, Clair. "Success with Natural Succession." Landscape Architecture, July 2004, pp. 60-63.
"2003 ASLA Awards." Landscape Architecture, September 2003, pp. 70-81.
"Bogs and Promenades Win Design Awards." Daily Journal of Commerce, November 26, 2003.
"ASLA to Honor Two Seattle Firms." Daily Journal of Commerce, July 1, 2003.
Kay, Jane Holtz. "Thinking Like and Urban Park." Landscape Architecture, October 2003, pp.210-212.
Freeman, Allen. "Out of This World." Landscape Architecture, October 2003, pp.68-79.
Benson, Don. "Seattle's Best Outdoor Spaces." Daily Journal of Commerce, April 10, 2003.
Enlow, Clair. "Zig Zag Art on a Green Carpet: A Sculpture Park to Unfold on the Seattle Waterfront." Landscape Architecture, vol. 92, no. 8, August 2002, pp. 22-23.
Bennett, Sam. "Snapshot: Charles Anderson." Daily Journal of Commerce, October 2, 2002.
Seven, Richard. "Around Every Turn, Discovery in Seattle's Largest Park." The Seattle Times, August 11, 2002.
Keeny, Gavin. On the Nature of Things: Contemporary American Landscape Architecture. Birkhauser, 2000, pp. 34-45.
Enlow, Clair. "Seattle Standoff." Landscape Architecture, October 2000, pp. 172, 169.
"Seattle, Silo's and Salmon: What to Do About 'Whoops." Architectural Record, June 2000.
"Mount St. Helens: Super-Real Reclamation." Landscape Architecture, February 1994.
Leccese, Michael. "Volcanic Ventures." Landscape Architecture, February 1993, pp. 38-43.
"Under the Volcano." Landscape Architecture, June 1991.

SELECTED AWARDS & HONORS

Cooper Hewitt, nominated National Design Award, 2009
5th European Biennial of Landscape Architecture, Barcelona Spain, Exhibition: "New American Landscape," Featuring the Olympic Sculpture Park, 2008
World Architecture Festival, Category Winner: Nature, Olympic Sculpture Park, 2008
EDRA/Places Awards, Olympic Sculpture Park, 2008
Travel + Leisure Design Awards: Best Cultural Space, Olympic Sculpture Park 2008
ASLA Washington Merit Award, Anchorage Museum Expansion, 2008
Veronica Rudge Green Prize in Urban Design, Harvard Design School, Olympic Sculpture Park, 2007
"Top Ten Best (New and Upcoming) Architectural Marvels." Time, Featuring The Olympic Sculpture Park, December, 2007_AIA National Honor Award, Olympic Sculpture Park, 2007
ASLA National Honor Award, Olympic Sculpture Park, 2007
AIA New York Excellence in Design Award, Olympic Sculpture Park, 2007
AIA New York Honor Award, New York Chapter AIA, Olympic Sculpture Park, 2007
AIA Seattle Honor Award, Olympic Sculpture Park, 2007
Finalist: International Urban, Landscape Award, Topos, A&W, Eurohypo, Olympic Sculpture Park, 2007
ASLA National Merit Award, Tables of Water, 2006
ASLA Washington Honor Award, Satsop Nuclear Gardens, 2006
Seattle Design Commission Award and Mayor Commendation, Olympic Sculpture Park, 2005
Groundswell Exhibit featuring Olympic Sculpture Park – MoMA, New York, 2005
First Place, Bellingham Children and Art Museum Design Competition, 2005
ASLA National Honor Award, Mount St. Helens National Volcanic Visitor Centers, 2005
ASLA Washington Honor Award, SATSOP, 2005
ASLA National Merit Award, The Trillium Projects, 2004
ASLA National Merit Award, Arthur Ross Terrace, 2003
ASLA Washington Merit Award, Roxhill Bog, 2003
ASLA Washington Merit Award, 500 Area of Discovery Park, 2003
ASLA Washington Merit Award, Lake Washington Environmental Education Sequence, 2003
Progressive Architecture Award, Architecture, Olympic Sculpture Park, 2003

PHOTOGRAPH CREDITS

#	PROJECT NAME	Photo location	Photo Credits
	Charles Headshot	Acknowledgents	Studio No. 5
	John E. Jaqua Academic Center for Student Athletes	Introduction 1	Wolfram Burner
	The Gardens of the Olympic Sculpture Park	Introduction 2	Bruce C. Moore
1	**The Visitor Centers at Mount St. Helens National Volcanic Monument**	26 top	USFS - United States Forest Service
		26 bottom	USFS - United States Forest Service
		27	Andrew Buchanan, Subtle Light Photography
		28 top	Andrew Buchanan, Subtle Light Photography
		28 bottom	Charles Anderson | Atelier ps
		29 site plans	Charles Anderson | Atelier ps
		29 top right	EDAW/Strode-Eckert Photography
		29 bottom right	Andrew Buchanan, Subtle Light Photography
		30	Andrew Buchanan, Subtle Light Photography
		31 top	Andrew Buchanan, Subtle Light Photography
		31 bottom	Andrew Buchanan, Subtle Light Photography
		32 top	Andrew Buchanan, Subtle Light Photography
		32 bottom	EDAW/Strode-Eckert Photography
		33 top	Andrew Buchanan, Subtle Light Photography
		33 bottom	Andrew Buchanan, Subtle Light Photography
2	**Arthur Ross Terrace, Museum of Natural History**	34	Charles Anderson | Atelier ps
		35	D Finnin/AMNH
		36	Nicole Beattie Vallespir
		37 top right	Nicole Beattie Vallespir
		37 top left	Nicole Beattie Vallespir
		37 bottom	Nicole Beattie Vallespir
		38 top	D Finnin/AMNH
		38 bottom	D Finnin/AMNH
		39 top	Nicole Beattie Vallespir
		39 bottom	Nicole Beattie Vallespir
		40	Nicole Beattie Vallespir
		41	Nicole Beattie Vallespir
3	**Satsop Development Park**	42 top	Charles Anderson | Atelier ps
		42 bottom	Charles Anderson | Atelier ps
		43	Charles Anderson Landscape Architecture
		44	Brice Maryman
		45	Charles Anderson
		46 top	Satsop Development Park
		46 bottom	Charles Anderson | Atelier ps
		47	Satsop Development Park
4	**Trillium Projects:**	49 (photo collage)	Charles Anderson | Atelier ps, Michelle Arab and Andrew Buchanan (Subtle Light Photography)
	Seward Park Native Plant Garden	50 top	Andrew Buchanan, Subtle Light Photography
		50 bottom left	Charles Anderson | Atelier ps
		50 bottom	Michelle Arab
		51	Andrew Buchanan, Subtle Light Photography
	Genesee Meadow	52 top	Charles Anderson | Atelier ps
		52 bottom right	Charles Anderson | Atelier ps
		52 bottom left	Charles Anderson | Atelier ps
		53	Michelle Arab
	Pritchard Beach Wetland Park	54 site plan	Charles Anderson | Atelier ps
		54 bottom right	Andrew Buchanan, Subtle Light Photography
		54 bottom left	Andrew Buchanan, Subtle Light Photography
		55 top	Andrew Buchanan, Subtle Light Photography
		55 bottom	Michelle Arab
	Colman Park	56 top	Charles Anderson | Atelier ps
		56 bottom	Andrew Buchanan, Subtle Light Photography
		57 top	Andrew Buchanan, Subtle Light Photography
		57 bottom	Andrew Buchanan, Subtle Light Photography
		58	Andrew Buchanan, Subtle Light Photography
		59	Andrew Buchanan, Subtle Light Photography
	Roxhill Bog	60 top	Charles Anderson | Atelier ps
		60 bottom right	Andrew Buchanan, Subtle Light Photography
		60 bottom left	Charles Anderson | Atelier ps
		61 top	Andrew Buchanan, Subtle Light Photography
		61 bottom right	Andrew Buchanan, Subtle Light Photography
		61 bottom left	Andrew Buchanan, Subtle Light Photography
	500 Area Discovery Park	62 top	Andrew Buchanan, Subtle Light Photography
		62 middle	Charles Anderson | Atelier ps
		62 bottom	Andrew Buchanan, Subtle Light Photography
		63	Andrew Buchanan, Subtle Light Photography

5	**Little Big House**	64 top	Charles Anderson | Atelier ps
		64 bottom	Philip Vogelzang
		65	Philip Vogelzang
		66 top	Charles Anderson | Atelier ps
		66 bottom	Philip Vogelzang
		67	Philip Vogelzang
		68 top	Philip Vogelzang
		68 bottom	Philip Vogelzang
		69 top	Philip Vogelzang
		69 bottom	Philip Vogelzang
		70	Philip Vogelzang
		71 top	Philip Vogelzang
		71 bottom	Philip Vogelzang
6	**Beijing 2008 Olympics Competition**	72	XWHO Design
		73 top	XWHO Design
		73 bottom plans	XWHO Design
7	**Kingdoms of Discovery**	74 top	Charles Anderson | Atelier ps
		74 bottom	Discoveryland, China
		75 top	Discoveryland, China
		75 bottom	Discoveryland, China
8	**Waterfront Place**	76 top	Charles Anderson | Atelier ps
		76 bottom	Charles Anderson | Atelier ps
		77 top	Charles Anderson | Atelier ps and Carlos Zapata Studio
		77 bottom	Charles Anderson | Atelier ps and Carlos Zapata Studio
9	**Madison Art House**	78 top	Charles Anderson | Atelier ps
		78 bottom	Domestic Architecture
		79	Charles Anderson | Atelier ps
		80	Charles Anderson | Atelier ps
		81	Charles Anderson | Atelier ps
		82	Domestic Architecture
		83	Charles Anderson | Atelier ps
		84 top	Charles Anderson | Atelier ps
		84 bottom	Charles Anderson | Atelier ps
		85	Charles Anderson | Atelier ps
		86	Charles Anderson | Atelier ps
		87	Charles Anderson | Atelier ps
		88	Charles Anderson | Atelier ps
		89	Charles Anderson | Atelier ps
		90	Charles Anderson | Atelier ps
		91	Charles Anderson | Atelier ps
		92-93	Charles Anderson | Atelier ps
10	**Tables of Water**	94 top	Charles Anderson | Atelier ps
		94 bottom	Michelle Arab
		95	Olson Kundig Architects
		96 top	Charles Anderson | Atelier ps
		96 bottom	Charles Anderson | Atelier ps
		97	Charles Anderson | Atelier ps
		98-99	Charles Anderson | Atelier ps
		100 top	Charles Anderson | Atelier ps
		100 bottom	Charles Anderson | Atelier ps
		101 top	Charles Anderson | Atelier ps
		101 bottom right	Charles Anderson | Atelier ps
		101 bottom left	Charles Anderson | Atelier ps
		102 top	Charles Anderson | Atelier ps
		102 bottom right	Charles Anderson | Atelier ps
		102 bottom left	Charles Anderson | Atelier ps
		103 top	Charles Anderson | Atelier ps
		103 bottom	Charles Anderson | Atelier ps
11	**Gardens of the Olympic Sculpture Park**	104 top	Charles Anderson | Atelier ps
		104 bottom	Lydia Heard
		105	Andrew Buchanan, Subtle Light Photography
		106	Andrew Buchanan, Subtle Light Photography
		107 top left	Charles Anderson
		107 plans and section	Charles Anderson | Atelier ps
		107 bottom	Andrew Buchanan, Subtle Light Photography
		108	Bruce C. Moore
		109	Andrew Buchanan, Subtle Light Photography
		110 top	Bruce C. Moore
		110 bottom	Ben Benschneider
		111	Arion Ellis Potts
		112-113	Charles Anderson
		114 top right	Thomas Brown

	114 top left	Andrew Buchanan, Subtle Light Photography
	114 bottom	Bruce C. Moore
	115 top	Lydia Heard
	115 bottom	Charles Anderson | Atelier ps
	116 top	Bruce C. Moore
	116 bottom	Bruce C. Moore
	116-117 middle	Charles Anderson | Atelier ps
	117 top	Bruce C. Moore
	117 middle	Bruce C. Moore
	117 bottom	Bruce C. Moore
	118	Lydia Heard
	119 top	Charles Anderson | Atelier ps
	119 bottom	Jeff Soderquist
12 **Whatcom Museum Light-catcher**	121	Olson Kundig Architects
	122 top	Olson Kundig Architects
	122 bottom right	Jeremy Smith
	122 bottom left	Tim Bies
	123 top	Peter James
	123 bottom	Charles Anderson | Atelier ps
	124 top	Peter James
	124 bottom left	Charles Anderson | Atelier ps
	124 bottom right	Bruce C. Moore
	125 top	XWHO Design
	125 bottom	Charles Anderson | Atelier ps
13 **Denver Art House**	126 top	Charles Anderson | Atelier ps
	126 bottom	Charles Anderson | Atelier ps
	127	Charles Anderson | Atelier ps
	128	Charles Anderson | Atelier ps
	129 top	Charles Anderson | Atelier ps
	129 bottom	Charles Anderson | Atelier ps
	130 top	Charles Anderson | Atelier ps
	130 bottom	Charles Anderson | Atelier ps
	131 top	Charles Anderson | Atelier ps
	131 bottom	Charles Anderson | Atelier ps
	132 top	Charles Anderson | Atelier ps
	132 bottom	Charles Anderson | Atelier ps
	133 top	Charles Anderson | Atelier ps
	133 bottom	Charles Anderson | Atelier ps
	134 top	Charles Anderson | Atelier ps
	134 bottom	Charles Anderson | Atelier ps
	135 left	Charles Anderson | Atelier ps
	135 top	Charles Anderson | Atelier ps
	135 middle	Charles Anderson | Atelier ps
	135 bottom	Charles Anderson | Atelier ps
14 **Hanoi Hotel and Convention Center**	136 top	Charles Anderson | Atelier ps
	136 bottom	Charles Anderson | Atelier ps and Carlos Zapata Studio
	137 top	Charles Anderson | Atelier ps and Carlos Zapata Studio
	137 bottom	Charles Anderson | Atelier ps and Carlos Zapata Studio
	138	Carlos Zapata Studio
	139 top	Carlos Zapata Studio
	139 bottom	Charles Anderson | Atelier ps and Carlos Zapata Studio
15 **University of Oregon: John E. Jaqua Academic Center for Student Athletes**	140 top	Wolfram Burner
	140 bottom	Charles Anderson | Atelier ps
	141	Kevin Clark
	142	Peter Eckert / Eckert & eckert
	143 top	Scott Scriven
	143 bottom	Andika Murandi
	144	Peter Eckert / Eckert & eckert
	145	Peter Eckert / Eckert & eckert
	146 top	Andika Murandi
	146 bottom left	Steven Pfaffle
	146 bottom right	Peter Eckert / Eckert & eckert
	147 top	Wolfram Burner
	147 bottom	Richard Gorecki
	148 top	Erik Bishoff
	148 bottom	Wolfram Burner
	149	Charles Anderson
16 **Zhongkai Sheshan Villas (Shanghai Villas)**	150 top	Charles Anderson | Atelier ps
	150 bottom	Charles Anderson | Atelier ps and XWHO Design
	151	XWHO Design
	152 top	Charles Anderson | Atelier ps
	152 bottom	Charles Anderson | Atelier ps
	153 top	XWHO Design
	153 bottom	XWHO Design

17 **Chapel in the Woods**	154 top	Charles Anderson | Atelier ps
	154 bottom left	Charles Anderson | Atelier ps and Tadao Ando Architects & Associates
	154 bottom right	Charles Anderson | Atelier ps and Tadao Ando Architects & Associates
	155	Tadao Ando Architects & Associates
18 **The Anchorage Common**	156 top	David Chipperfield Architects
	156 bottom	Ken Graham Photography
	157	Ken Graham Photography
	158 top	Ken Graham Photography
	158 bottom	Ken Graham Photography
	159 top	Charles Anderson | Atelier ps
	159 bottom	Charles Anderson | Atelier ps
	160 top	Ken Graham Photography
	160 bottom	Charles Anderson
	161 top	Ken Graham Photography
	161 bottom	Ken Graham Photography
	162 top	Ken Graham Photography
	162 bottom	Ken Graham Photography
	163	Ken Graham Photography
	164 top	Charles Anderson | Atelier ps
	164 bottom	Charles Anderson | Atelier ps
	165	Ken Graham Photography
	166	Ken Graham Photography
	167 top	Ken Graham Photography
	167 bottom	Charles Anderson | Atelier ps
19 **International Peace Garden United States and Canada**	168	Charles Anderson | Atelier ps
	169	Charles Anderson | Atelier ps
	170	Charles Anderson | Atelier ps
	171 top	International Peace Garden
	171 bottom	Charles Anderson | Atelier ps
	172 top	Charles Anderson | Atelier ps
	172 bottom	Charles Anderson | Atelier ps
	173 all pictures	Charles Anderson | Atelier ps
	174	Charles Anderson | Atelier ps
	175	Charles Anderson | Atelier ps
20 **Lean Linear City/Paolo Soleri**	177	Charles Anderson | Atelier ps and Arcosanti Foundation
	178	Charles Anderson | Atelier ps and Arcosanti Foundation
	179 top	Charles Anderson | Atelier ps and Arcosanti Foundation
	179 bottom	Charles Anderson | Atelier ps and Arcosanti Foundation
	180 top	Charles Anderson | Atelier ps and Arcosanti Foundation
	180 bottom	Charles Anderson | Atelier ps and Arcosanti Foundation
	181 all pictures	Charles Anderson | Atelier ps and Arcosanti Foundation
	182-183	Charles Anderson | Atelier ps and Arcosanti Foundation
21 **Hangzhou CBD**	184 top	Charles Anderson | Atelier ps
	184 bottom	XWHO Design
	184	XWHO Design
	186	XWHO Design
	187	XWHO Design
22 **Fraternal Twins**	188 top	Charles Anderson | Atelier ps
	188 bottom	Charles Anderson | Atelier ps
	189	Charles Anderson | Atelier ps
	190-191	Charles Anderson | Atelier ps
23 **Inn at the Market Courtyard**	192 top	Michelle Arab
	192 bottom	Michelle Arab
	193	Michelle Arab
	194	Michelle Arab
	195 top	Michelle Arab
	195 bottom	Michelle Arab
24 **South Coast Plaza**	196 top	Charles Anderson | Atelier ps
	196 bottom	Charles Anderson | Atelier ps
	197	Charles Anderson | Atelier ps
	198	Charles Anderson | Atelier ps
	199 top	Charles Anderson | Atelier ps
	199 bottom	Charles Anderson | Atelier ps
	200 top	Charles Anderson | Atelier ps
	200 bottom	Charles Anderson | Atelier ps
	201 top	Charles Anderson | Atelier ps
	201 bottom	Charles Anderson | Atelier ps
25 **3031 Western Avenue**	202 top	Charles Anderson | Atelier ps
	202 bottom	Charles Anderson | Atelier ps
	203	Charles Anderson | Atelier ps and Hinthorn Mott Architects
	204	Charles Anderson | Atelier ps and Hinthorn Mott Architects
	205	Charles Anderson | Atelier ps and Hinthorn Mott Architects